TI

Foreword

Thank you so much for choosing this book!

Attention: This book is the sequel to the book "Arduino Projects with Tinkercad", as well as to the beginner book "Arduino | Step by Step". This book is aimed at advanced Arduino users and therefore requires some basic knowledge. It is best to work through the two books mentioned above before starting with this book.

In this book we will create together and step by step a few complex and great projects with the microcontroller Arduino Uno. As in the previous book, we will use the easy-to-use and free online software Tinkercad from Autodesk to simulate and program the projects. In Tinkercad, we will create - together and step by step - the schematic for each project, create the programming using the block-based programming method, and simulate how it works. In each of the projects we will use sensors, e.g. a force sensor, a tilt sensor, a soil moisture sensor or an ambient light sensor and other components. In addition, we will integrate actuators (servo motor, piezo ...) that will perform a specific programmed action.

I am an engineer (M.Eng.) and would like to introduce you to the topics of electronics, Arduino and block-based programming with Tinkercad, application-oriented, playful and simply explained using DIY projects. Therefore, you will find in this book in the first two chapters a very short refresher about the Arduino and the program Tinkercad (about 5 pages). If you need a more detailed introduction, you should take a look at the previous books in this series. After that, five more complex projects will follow, which we will implement together and step by step (components, schematic, wiring, programming). Let's go!

2

Table of contents

1 Scope of learning

What you can expect in this book and what you will learn

In this guide you will find five exciting and great projects that we will implement together and step by step. These projects are a bit more complex, as this book is intended for advanced users. For the electronic projects we use the microcontroller Arduino, as well as the software Tinkercad from Autodesk. In the first two chapters you will find a very short refresher on the Arduino and the Tinkercad program (about 5 pages). If you need a more detailed introduction, you should take a look at the previous books in this series, whose titles are mentioned in the preface.

In this book, you will also be asked in places to carry out individual steps or even an entire project on your own. The solution will follow on the following pages. Try to implement these prompts, then you learn best!

This book includes the following projects:

- DIY project 1: car folding headlight with automatic low beam
- DIY project 2: Complex alarm system with various sensors
- DIY project 3: Plant monitoring and supply
- DIY project 4: Parking aid and garage air monitoring
- DIY Project 5: Mini Piano

2 What is an Arduino? | Refresh old knowledge

Simply put, an Arduino is nothing more than a small and very simple mini-PC or microcontroller that is capable of receiving input signals, processing them internally and then converting them into corresponding output signals. An input signal could be e.g. sunlight falling on a sensor. The corresponding output signal could e.g. control a (blind) motor. There are different models of the Arduino. For our projects in this book we only need the Arduino UNO (https://www.arduino.cc/en/main/products).

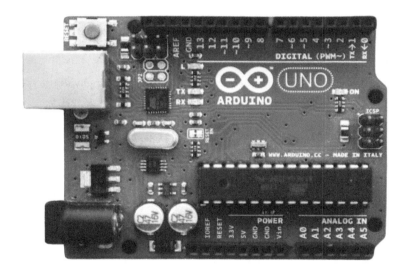

How does an Arduino work? The basic principle behind every PC is the binary system based on the two numbers "0" (OFF) and "1" (ON). Communication takes place in a PC with combinations of these two numbers. Exactly this principle is also used in the Arduino. The two binary numbers are represented here by the voltages 5V ("1" or "HIGH" value) and 0V ("0" or "LOW" value). Each pin on an Arduino board is assigned a number or label. There are several digital and analog pins that can receive and send signals. You can connect sensors or other components, such as a motor, to these pins. The board works with 5V direct current. The Arduino also has a processor that can be programmed to execute desired commands.

3 What is Tinkercad? | Refresh old knowledge

Tinkercad is an online platform of the company Autodesk, where you can realize projects of a technical nature. The term "Tinker" means something like tinkering or fiddling. "CAD" stands for "Computer-Aided Design". With Tinkercad you can work on electronics projects, program and also create 3D objects. Creating 3D objects is not part of this book.

Since Tinkercad is an online software, you can't and don't have to download the software, but you can simply work in your preferred browser. In addition, Tinkercad can be used free of charge. Based on its appearance, Tinkercad's target group can mainly be identified as children and teenagers. In my opinion, however, the program is also excellent for adults, especially if you are a beginner. Just this simplicity offers many advantages and quick success in dealing with the creation of 3D objects or electronic circuits.

All projects are stored in the cloud and so you can access them from anywhere with a computer, cell phone or tablet via the Internet.

Create an account and get started

Before we can start creating our projects, we must first create an account on the www.tinkercad.com website. If we already have an account with Autodesk, we can use it to log in. Otherwise, we can either register with a Google account or Apple account, or - quite classically - with an email address.

As soon as you have logged in, you can view and copy the project online in Tinkercad using the respective link of the project (you can find the link at the beginning of the chapter "Required components"). However, it is best to do this only after you have created the projects yourself, or only if you are stuck at a certain point. Otherwise you will not have a good learning effect.

In order to design electronic circuits in Tinkercad, we need to be in the "Designs" section **(2)** on the start page **(1)**.

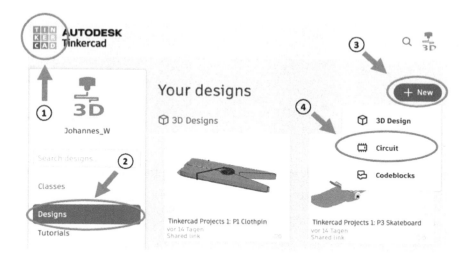

Here we can create a new circuit with "+ New" **(3)** and "Circuit" **(4)**.

Once we have created a new "Circuit" project, the workspace for creating electrotechnical circuits opens.

The gray area is our work plane where we design our circuits. With the help of the mouse wheel, you can use the zoom function. You can also move the components by holding down the left mouse button, holding down the right mouse button, or holding down the mouse wheel.

On the right side are all available electronic components, e.g. an LED, a resistor, a switch, a capacitor or a battery. There is also a search function and the possibility to display more components (switch from "Basic" to "All" in the dropdown menu).

In addition, you can switch to another arrangement, the list view, with the small list icon in the upper right corner. Just try it out. In the list view you also get a short description of each component.

At the top right, you can display the circuit diagram or the parts list of the project. With "Code" you can switch to the programming view and with "Start Simulation" you can virtually test the function of the project.

Fantastic! Now we have briefly refreshed our background knowledge of the Arduino and Tinkercad and can start acquiring new knowledge. We will do this in the following in a playful way using the illustrative DIY projects. As in the first part of this book series, we will again mainly work with block-based programming in Tinkercad, because it offers a simple and great approach. Occasionally, however, we will also take a look at text-based code. Let's go !

4 Project 1 | Folding headlights with automatic low beam

For this project, we imagine the low beam of a car. In a modern car, the low beam switches on and off depending on the ambient light. For example, the low beam switches on when it gets dark outside and switches off again when it is bright outside. Depending on the design, this is also the case when driving into or out of a tunnel. We would like to simulate this function with an Arduino in our first project. For this purpose, we use an ambient light sensor. An ambient light sensor monitors the light that falls on the sensor and gives us feedback whether it is currently light or dark in the environment. By the way, such a sensor is also built into most modern smartphones so that the screen brightness can automatically adjust to the ambient light.

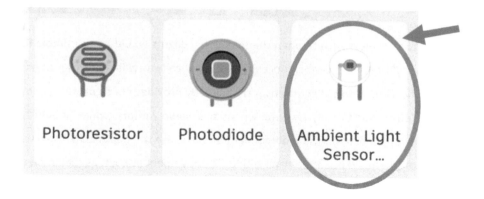

However, we now not only want the two low beams, which are symbolized by two white LEDs in our project, to turn on or off when it gets dark or bright, but we even want to control the brightness of the LEDs depending on the ambient light. This means that the LEDs should shine brightest when it is darkest outside and only shine very dimly when it is bright outside. In between, the brightness should vary continuously.

The current brightness of the LEDs should also be displayed on the car's dashboard using an LCD screen. When the LEDs are at full brightness - that is, when it is darkest outside - the display should be filled in as follows: ##########, on the other hand, when the LEDs are only dimly lit, only a few: ## should appear.

To make the project a bit more complex, we don't want to install simple low beam headlights in our car, but flip-up headlights. This type of headlight is sometimes found on older sports cars. These headlights flip open when you press a switch.

However, a simple switch to open the folding headlights would be too simple for us. We would rather have this process go automatically as well. For this purpose, we use the same ambient light sensor that already provides our signal for the low beam control. Additionally, we implement two servo motors, which should be controlled depending on the ambient light and execute the flap mechanism. The servo motors should open the flaps with a 90° movement as soon as the ambient light gets darker and close them again as soon as it is bright enough. The flap should therefore open as soon as dusk falls outside and close again as soon as it is light outside.

This sounds a bit more complex at first, especially because several processes have to run at once. But don't worry, we will find a solution together, step by step and in detail. Let's first take a look at which components we need for this project, how we need to wire them, and then we'll get down to programming.

4.1 Required components

Link to the Tinkercad project: https://bit.ly/3Rgdnel

Quantity	Designation
1	Arduino Uno
1	Breadboard (small)
1	Ambient light sensor
2	LEDs (white)
2	100 Ω resistors for LEDs
1	80 kΩ resistor for ambient light sensor
2	Servo motor
1	LCD display 16×2 **(I2C and MCP23008 based)**

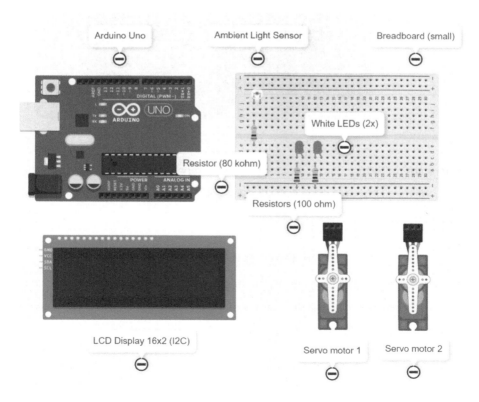

Notes on the LCD display 16×2 (I2C):

In this project we use an LCD display with 16 rows and 2 lines (16×2) of the I2C type. I2C means "Inter-Integrated Circuit" and stands for a communication method. Compared to the also available normal 16×2 LCD display without the addition of I2C, it is easier to wire because it has only four connections instead of sixteen. Two of the four connectors on the I2C display are for power (GND "-" and VCC "+"), so only two connectors are needed for data communication (SDA and SCL). The SCL connector is used to receive the clock signal and the SDA connector is used to transmit the data bits. The type shall be a MCP23008 based display (click on display to edit).

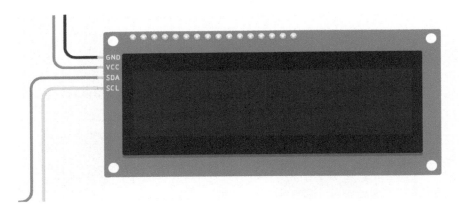

There are no further details about the other components at this point, since they are resistors, LEDs and servo motors. We have already covered these sufficiently in the first book of the series.

4.2 The design of the circuit diagram

In this chapter we will design the circuit diagram of our system or take a closer look at it. In the following we will first have a look at the schematic view of the required circuit diagram. In the next step, we will then build the circuit 1:1.

Schematic circuit diagram:

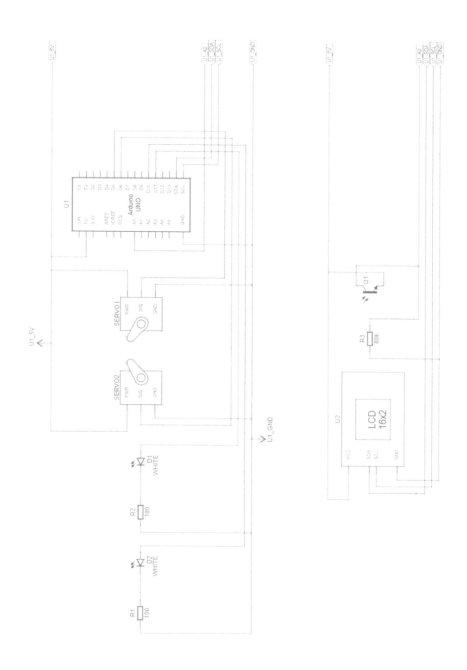

To build the circuit in Tinkercad, we start with the breadboard as the starting point in the middle of the circuit. To do this, we switch from "Basic" to "All" in the right menu bar at "Components" to have all components available. Alternatively, we can also use the search function.

First we need an ambient light sensor which we place in the upper left corner of the breadboard. We also need a 80 kΩ resistor for this sensor. Furthermore we add two white LEDs (select red LED in the components and then change color to white) with a 100 Ω resistor each.

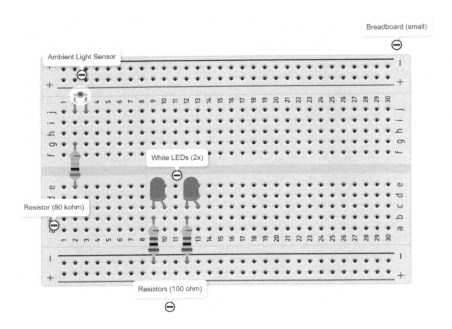

In the next step, we place an Arduino Uno to the left of the breadboard and connect our previously placed components. For this we put a blue connection from the ambient light sensor to the analog input A0 of the Arduino. This connection provides us with the signal. Our ambient light sensor is a simple phototransistor (combination of photodiode and transistor; for higher currents compared to the photodiode), which has an emitter terminal (E) and a collector terminal (C). We connect the positive terminal (5V) of our power source (Arduino board) to the

14

emitter (E) and the negative terminal (GND) through the resistor to the collector of the sensor. The LEDs are already connected to the negative terminal of the board for proper resistor placement at their cathode (-). We connect the two anodes of the LEDs (+) to the Arduino pin 10 and 11 respectively. Finally we supply the breadboard with power by placing a black wire between "GND" and "-", and a red wire between 5V and "+".

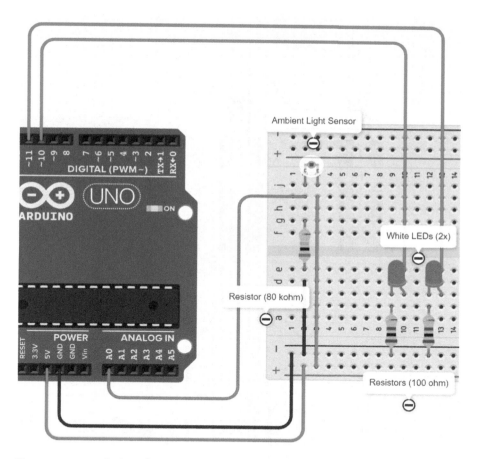

Now we are missing the connections between Arduino and display and the connections for the servo motors. The servo motors have three connections. Two of them are for the power supply (VCC: "+" and GND: "-") and one of them is for the control signal. We connect the servo motors to the power supply of the breadboard and put one purple signal line each to the Arduino pins 5 and 6 respectively. We also connect the display to the power supply of the breadboard first. We connect the two signal lines (SDA and SCL) to the very top left (next to the digital PINs as well as GND and AREF) of the Arduino. These two pins of the Ardunio are for SDA and SCL, but unfortunately they are not labeled here (there is a label in the schematic).

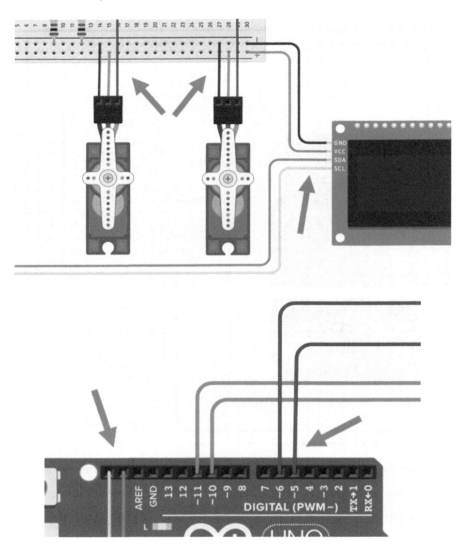

Complete circuit diagram:

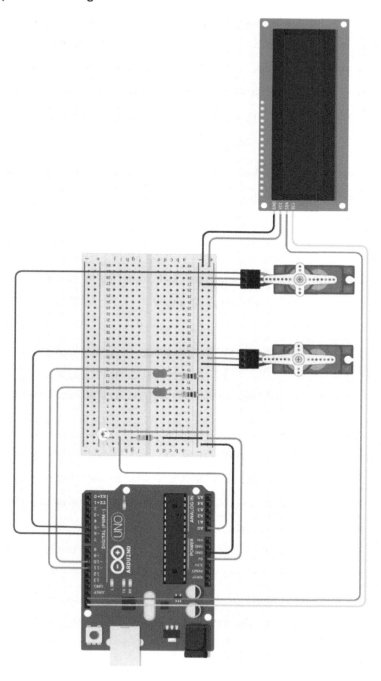

4.3 Development of the program code

After we have successfully wired our first project, the next step is to get started with the required programming. For this we use - as already mentioned - the block-based programming in Tinkercad. In order to start programming, we switch to the programming window by clicking the "Code" button in the upper right corner. In addition, we select "Blocks" in the drop-down menu and delete all already existing blocks.

As we learned in the first book of the series, block-based programming can basically always consist of three blocks: "title block comment" (optional), "on start", and "forever".

Step 1:

In the first step we create the optional title block (found in the "Notation" category) and write the text "automatic headlights" into it.

Step 2:

In the second step, we add a block called "on start", which can be found in the "Control" section in Tinkercad. This block is similar to the "Setup" section in a simple Arduino code. The block is used to execute a certain line of code only once at program start. What code do we need to have executed only once in this project? The initialization of the LCD display. We do that with the "configure LCD" command from the "Output" category. Since we have only one LCD display, it has the number 1 and the address 32. The type of the display is: I2C MCP23008. We can find this information by clicking on the display. We could also modify them here as we wish. I won't always map the previous blocks below for better viewing, you can just always place the blocks below the previous block.

Step 3:

Then, in the "Variables" category, we create the three variables: "light_val", "control" and "level".

From here on - if you want - you can also switch to the "Blocks + Text" view in the selection menu, so that you see not only the block code, but also the text code. On the one hand, this can be confusing - so you'd better switch back - on the other hand, it provides you with more information.

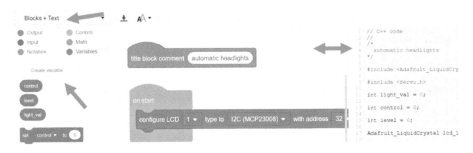

Step 4:

Now we need a "forever" block that contains the code to be executed in a loop (analogous to void loop () in text-based code).

Since we first need a signal with which we can control something afterwards, the first step here is to read the value of the ambient light sensor. We do this with "read analog pin A0" (connection pin of the sensor). We want to assign the value to the variable "light_val" with "set ... to ..." in the same step. Then we have to

19

convert the analog value that the sensor gives us (range 0 to 1023) into a digital value (0 to 255). We do this with the function "map ... to range ..." from the category "Math". We use the new variable "control" for this.

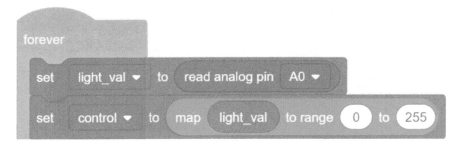

If you want to know even more about the function "map ()" or even other functions, you can read the detailed description of each function best online, directly at arduino.cc. Here is the link to the function "map": https://www.arduino.cc/reference/en/language/functions/math/map/

Step 5:

In this step we implement a control option for us as programmers. For example, we want the value that the sensor is currently measuring to be output to the serial monitor. For this we use the command "print to serial monitor ..." from the category "Output". We are currently and, in the following, still in the area "forever".

The value of the light sensor is then displayed to us in the serial monitor as follows (Light Value: -> analog measurement value -> digital value):

Serial Monitor
```
Light Value :   4/1
117
Light Value :   471
117
Light Value :   1009
251
```

Step 6:

After that we implement the calculation for the values of our LEDs. Let's briefly recall how this works. We want the LEDs to shine brightest when it is darkest outside. How can we implement this? With a very simple mathematical equation. We can drive the LEDs with the digital output pins 10 or 11 with a value between 0 and 255 (0 = no current flow, 255 = maximum current flow). Now we simply subtract the value that our sensor provides (after conversion to digital). That means, the LEDs are controlled with 255 - sensor value (variable: "control" for the digital value). If it is dark, the sensor delivers the value 0, i.e. 255 - 0 = 255 (LEDs shine maximum bright). If it is bright outside, the sensor delivers the analog value 1023, which we converted to 255 with "map". This means: 255 - 255 = 0 (LEDs do not shine). And in the range in between there is a stepless control. This is exactly what we wanted! In block codes it looks like this:

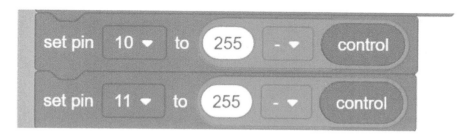

Step 7:

We have now already implemented the automatic low beam. Now we will deal with the two servo motors that are to control the folding mechanism of our headlights. For this we need an "if ... else" condition. We want the folding headlights to open at a certain brightness. For this we use the variable "control", which gives us the brightness value (0-255). Now we can define a value from which the folding lights should open, this can be the value "100" for example. But you can also choose another one, if this is too dark or too bright for you. The following code block must now say the following: If the value for brightness exceeds the value of 100, then both servo motors should rotate to the position 90° (you could also use any other value, e.g. 180°). Otherwise (if the value remains below 100), the servo motors should rotate to position 0°. Try to implement this "if ... else" condition yourself, before you have a look at the picture (the solution).

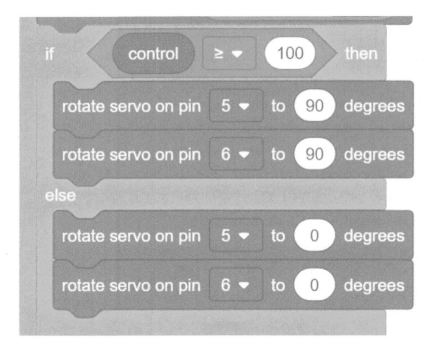

Step 8:

Perfect ! Now we are almost ready. We are still missing the indication of the luminous intensity of the LEDs on the display, which we could fix e.g. on the dashboard in the car. For this we have to set the position of the displayed text on the display on the one hand and on the other hand we have to set the text that should be displayed. We do this with "set position on LCD ..." and "print to LCD ...". In order to display the intensity in the form of one or more "#" symbols, we first have to map the sensor value of the ambient light sensor using the variable "level" and the function "map" (similar to step 4). We want to display 16 "#" symbols when the LEDs are fully luminous, so we need to convert the sensor values to the range 16 to -1. We need the -1 so that no "#" symbol is displayed at all when the LEDs are off or the ambient light is at maximum brightness. With 0 instead of -1 we would still get a "#" symbol displayed.

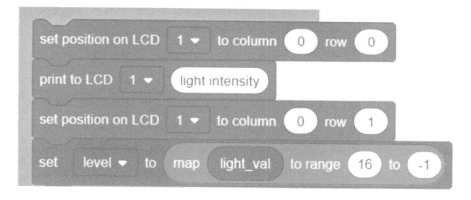

Step 9:

In this last step, we now implement two "for" loops that allow us to show the graduated intensity on the display. To do this, we use the "repeat" code block from the "Control" section twice. This is similar to a "for" loop in a text-based code. We want to display a "#" symbol ("print to LCD ...") as long as the internal count variable is below the value of the variable "levels". In simple terms, this means that first a # symbol is displayed, then another symbol in addition, i.e.: ## and then ###, and so on, until the number of symbols (internal count variable) equals the value of the variable level (converted ambient light intensity). To reverse this process when the LED luminosity is lower, we subtract a "#" symbol in another "for" loop ("repeat ...") until the display corresponds to the value of the variable.

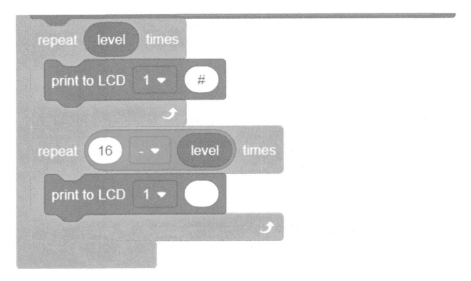

Perfect! Now we are done with the program code of the first project. Now it's time to try out the project in Tinkercad. To do so, start the simulation with the button "Start Simulation" and click on the ambient light sensor. A slider will appear with which you can simulate the intensity of the ambient light. Move the slider (slowly) from left to right and after a pause from right to left and see what happens. The system reacts a bit delayed, so you have to wait a few seconds until e.g. the values on the display are updated. In the following you will find the program code in an overall view:

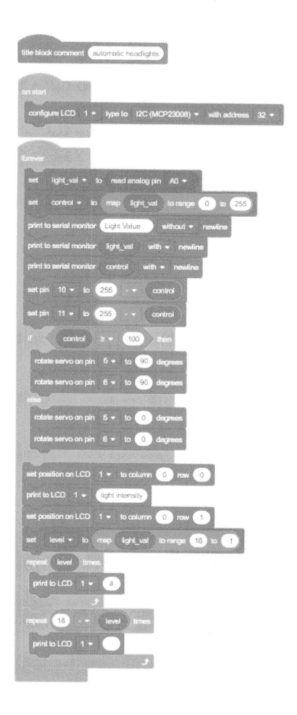

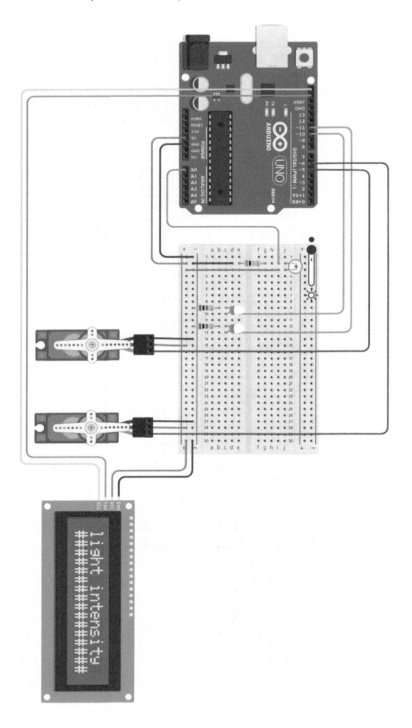

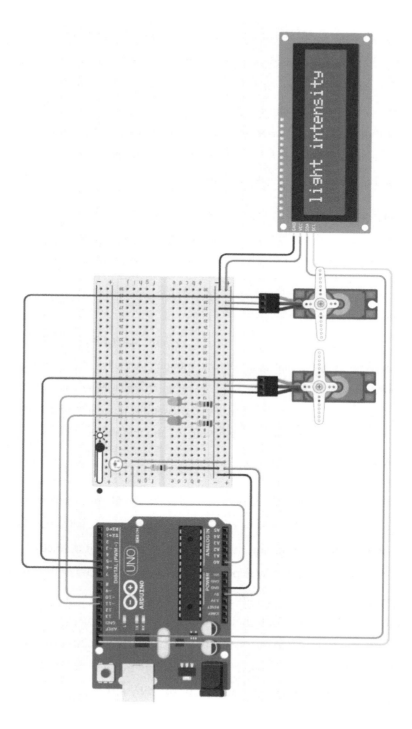

5 Project 2 | Alarm system with various sensors

In this project we will develop an alarm system. We will use two different types of sensors to detect intruders. First, we want to implement two motion sensors, each of which can detect motion in a separate room. Second, we will use two force sensors that send a signal when a force is applied to them. For example, the force sensor could be located under a doormat near a door and as soon as the burglar steps on the doormat, the sensor will register that.

If at least one of these four sensors (2x motion sensors and 2x force sensors) or even two or more of them detect a signal, an alarm shall be triggered. The acoustic alarm shall be generated by a piezo and the optical alarm by an alternate blinking of two red LEDs.

Refresher on the PIR sensor:

A PIR sensor ("Pyroelectric Infrared Sensor" or also "Passive Infrared Sensor") is a semiconductor device that can detect motion. Actually, the sensor detects temperature changes, which in turn result in voltage changes. When a living thing (body heat) or other heat source is detected within the sensing range, the sensor provides a digital "HIGH" signal (5V). We will see how to use the three connections in a moment with the circuit diagram.

However, the alarm should only be triggered when the alarm system is activated. Activation or deactivation must be possible by entering a code. In the case of block-based programming, we will enter this code via the serial monitor, since a "keypad" with block codes is not so easy to program. However, at the end of the project we will see how to add text-based programming to a "keypad" for entering the code. Also, two LEDs (green and red) should indicate the status of the alarm system. The green LED shall be on when the system is active, and the red LED shall be on when the alarm system is deactivated. In addition, on the display, the process of activation and deactivation shall be accompanied by a text (enter code; system active; enter code; system <u>not</u> active). For example, the code for activating the alarm system should be 0378493, and the code for deactivating it should be 2047291. However, it is possible to implement any other codes.

5.1 Required components

Link to the Tinkercad project: https://bit.ly/3yqcJCi

Quantity	Designation
1	Arduino Uno
1	Breadboard (small)
2	Force sensor
2	Motion detector (PIR sensor)
6	1 kΩ resistors
1	Piezo
1	LCD display 16×2 **(I2C and MCP23008 based)**
4	LEDs (3x red and 1x green)

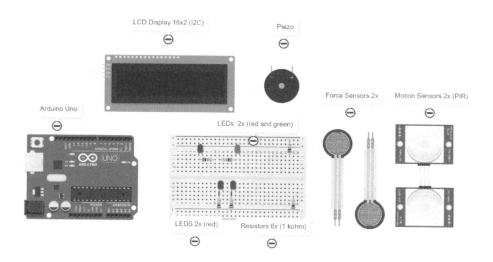

5.2 The design of the circuit diagram

First, we will again design the circuit diagram of our system. For this purpose in the following first the schematic view of the required circuit diagram:

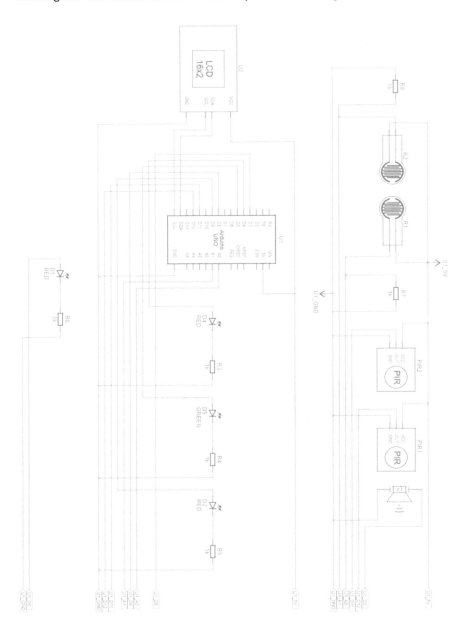

To build the circuit in Tinkercad, we start again with the breadboard as the starting point in the middle of the circuit. In addition, we change in the right menu bar at "Components" again from "Basic" to "All" to also find all components.

In the first step we position the LEDs and the resistors as shown. Make sure that especially the resistors are placed correctly. To supply the breadboard with power in the area above and below, we also lay black and red lines from the 5V and GND pin of the Arduino to the breadboard. Then we need a few more black wires to connect all components to ground (GND).

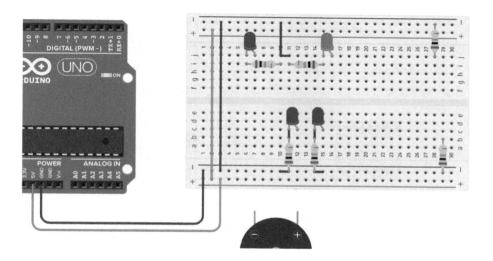

In the next step we connect all LEDs to the Arduino. We do this by creating a connection between the anode of each LED and a digital pin of the Arduino. We use the digital pins 4, 5, 8 and 9 for this. The colors of the wires (red, green, purple, pink) are not important for this by the way, but should be different to each other to keep or get a better overview or contrast to each other.

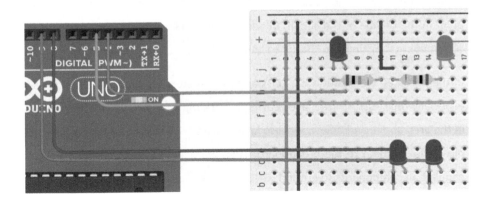

Then we supply the piezo buzzer that is supposed to generate our alarm sound. We simply connect the negative terminal of the piezo to the negative "-" pin line of the breadboard. We connect the positive terminal of the piezo to the digital pin 3 of the Arduino so that we can control the current flow through it.

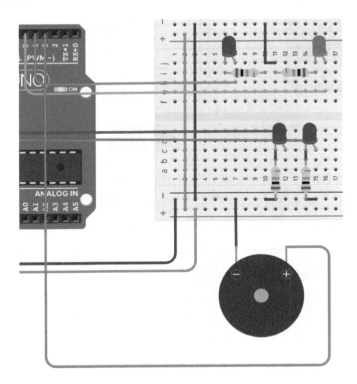

Now we connect the two force sensors with the breadboard and the Arduino. For this we connect one line (red) to the positive "+" pin line of the breadboard and the other line (black) to the breadboard, which in turn connects with another line (green or orange) to the analog Arduino pins A0 or A1. By the way, it doesn't matter which connection of the force sensor is used for which line.

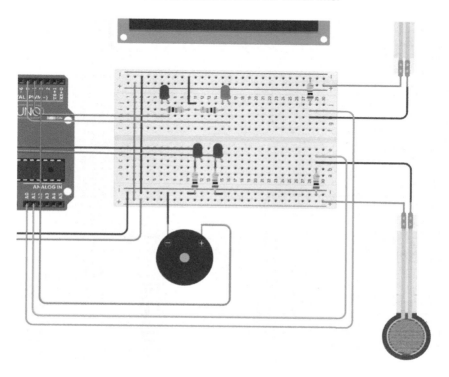

For the connection of the two motion detectors we proceed similarly. First we supply them with power (we need the two right pins for this; pin connection points downwards). Connect the right pin with "-" and the middle pin with "+".

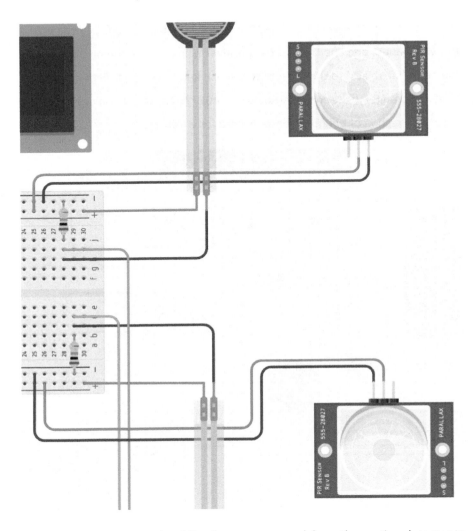

After that we connect a signal line (green or orange) from the motion detector to the digital Arduino pin 11 or 12. Finally we connect the LCD display in the usual way - like in the previous project. To do this, we supply it with power via the breadboard and connect the connections "SDA" and "SCL" of the display with the designated pins of the Arduino.

We can see these two steps on the following final schematic.

Complete circuit diagram:

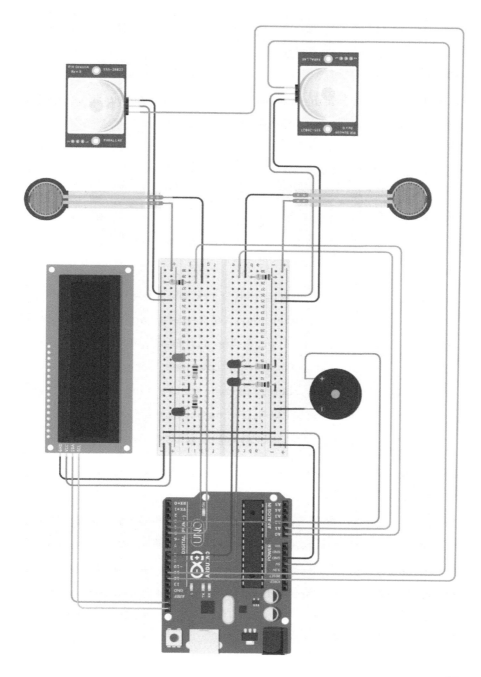

5.3 Development of the program code

After we have successfully wired our second project as well, we will get back to the required programming in this section.

Step 1:

In the first step we create the optional title block (found in the "Notation" category) with the text "alarm system".

Step 2:

In the second step, we add the "on start" block, which executes a certain line of code only once when the program starts. What code do we need to execute only once in this project? Think about the first project! Exactly, the initialization of the LCD display. We do that again with the command "configure LCD" from the category "Output". Number, address and type are like in the first project. I won't always show the preceding blocks here either for a better view in the following. You can simply place the following blocks again below the previous block.

But this step is not finished yet, because in this block we also want to show a start text on the display. We want to indicate that a code must be entered, and that the system is active.

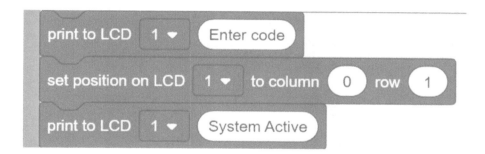

In addition, we don't want to just display it, we want the system to actually be active at startup. To do this, we first declare all the variables that we need in this project. We do that in the category "Variables".

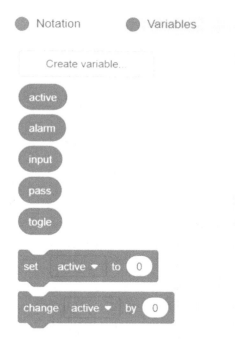

We need the three variables "active", "alarm" and "togle" already at startup. So that the system is active at startup, we set the variable "active" to the value 1 ("on"). We set the variable "alarm" to the value 0 ("off"), so that the alarm is off at system startup. We also set the variable "togle" to the value 1 ("on"). We will see later why we need this variable.

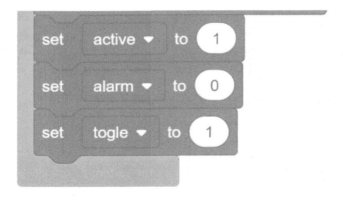

Step 3:

Now the "on start" block is done, and next we need another "forever" block that contains the code to be executed in a loop (analogous to void loop () in text-based code).

First we build in a small delay so that the Arduino has enough time to finish all previous processes. After that we set the variable "pass" to the value "0".

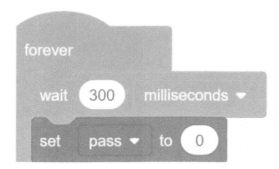

Now several if-conditions follow, which allow us to query the password or to compare the input in the serial monitor with the password.

By the way, we can open the serial monitor for later code input in the programming area:

Let's deal with the if-conditions now. First, we check if something was entered into the serial monitor. We do this with "number of serial characters available", which in normal text code corresponds to the function "Serial.available ()". For more information, see here:

https://www.arduino.cc/reference/en/language/functions/communication/serial/available/

The number of characters entered must be greater than 0, otherwise logically nothing was entered. After that we check with an if-else-condition ("if ... else" instead of a simple if-condition), if the number of entered characters is exactly 7 (our two codes have exactly 7 numbers each). We do this so that only seven-digit inputs are checked, because if the number of numbers is already not correct, you can save the check anyway.

Now it gets a bit more complex. We first have to convert the entered number from a char value (input format in the serial monitor) to a decimal value with the help of an ASCII table. An ASCII table can be found here, for example:

https://upload.wikimedia.org/wikipedia/commons/1/1b/ASCII-Table-wide.svg

The use of the table and the conversion (on the example of the code for the activation of the alarm system) is then done as follows:

Decimal	Hex	Char
40	28	(
41	29	)
42	2A	*
43	2B	+
44	2C	,
45	2D	-
46	2E	.
47	2F	/
48	30	0
49	31	1
50	32	2
51	33	3
52	34	4

char   0 3 7 8 4 9 3

deci   48 51 55 56 52 57 51

Then we implement an arithmetic operation. We want to add the converted input values to twice the previous sum. This means:

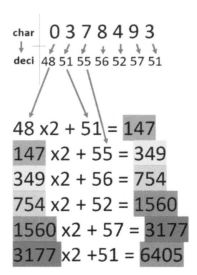

char   0 3 7 8 4 9 3

deci   48 51 55 56 52 57 51

$$48 \times 2 + 51 = 147$$
$$147 \times 2 + 55 = 349$$
$$349 \times 2 + 56 = 754$$
$$754 \times 2 + 52 = 1560$$
$$1560 \times 2 + 57 = 3177$$
$$3177 \times 2 + 51 = 6405$$

We do this in Tinkercad with the following formula:

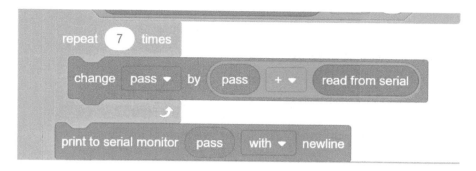

Step 4:

In this step, we must now first check whether the converted input (code) corresponds to the value 6405 (result of step 3 in red) or 6371 (value for converted code for deactivation; calculation analogous to step 3). We do this again with an if-else condition (select "if ... else"!). Why do we do this? So that only those cases are considered here in which one of the two codes was entered (incorrect entries are therefore not followed up in this section). Another if-check (question: Does the variable "pass" have the value 6405 for the activation?) follows. If this condition is fulfilled, then on the LCD display at the position 0 / 0 (row: 0, line: 0) the text "Enter Code" should be displayed and at the position 0 / 1, i.e. one line below, the text "System Active".

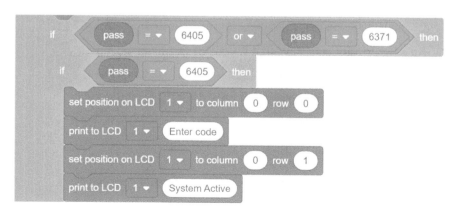

In addition, there is more to be done. First, we delete the last three characters shown in the second row on the display using a for loop (here: "repeat ... times") and "print to LCD" (no value here means overwrite value empty). Why this is necessary is hard to explain. You should try it at the end by deleting this block (make a copy of your project first) and simulate the transition between system active, system not active and again system active using the passwords.

On the other hand, our variable that reflects the state of the alarm system (active or not active) is to be set to the value 1 ("on" or active). And since we have installed two control LEDs, these should also be controlled here. The red LED should not light up (pin 4 "LOW"), but the green LED should light up (pin 5 "HIGH").

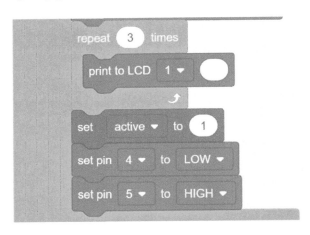

Now we have implemented everything for the activation of our alarm system by code. Be sure to stick with it, even if it's a bit more complex at first glance, soon we'll have the project done and ready to simulate! There's no shame in reading a few pages two or three times if you haven't understood something at first attempt. You can do it!

Step 5:

In this next step we will implement the opposite of the previous code, i.e. disabling the alarm system. First, we check with an if-condition whether the converted input (code) corresponds to the value 6371. If this check is true, then again the text "Enter code" and this time additionally "System not Active" shall be displayed. We also have to consider the positions on the LCD display here. In addition, the variable "active" should be set to the value 0 ("off"; system not active) and the pins for the red or green LED should be controlled accordingly (red: "HIGH"; green: "LOW"). We also need to turn off the alarm in case it is currently reporting an intrusion, but the system is disabled with the correct code. We do this by setting the variable "alarm" to the value 0 ("off").

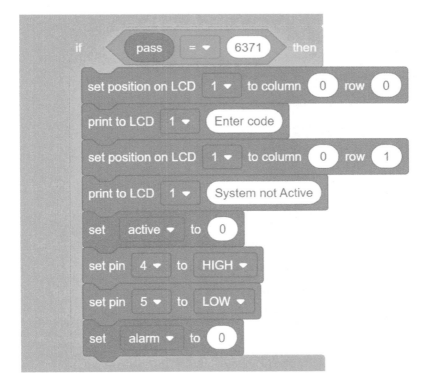

Step 6:

In the following, we are now in the else sections of the if-else conditions from step 3 and step 4 (blocks again seamlessly connect to step 5).

If the verification in step 3 (input has more or less than 7 characters) is not successful, the text: "wrong pass" should be displayed, because then the entered password is wrong. The same should happen if the verification in step 4 (converted input (code) corresponds to the value 6405 or 6371) is not successful.

By the way, with "set input ..." and "read from serial" we still define that the variable "input" reads and gets assigned the value from the serial monitor.

We now have to define what should happen when the alarm system is activated. In this case, the sensor values are to be read out and if one of them exceeds or has reached a certain threshold (analog value of the force sensor greater than 70 = approx. 0.3 -0.4 N; digital value of the motion sensor at 1 for "motion detected"), then the variable "alarm" is to be activated (value 1 = "on"), otherwise it is to be deactivated (value 0 = "off"). We implement this with an if-condition and an if-else-condition as follows.

The following original image is divided into two images below for better readability:

Original:

Split for better readability:

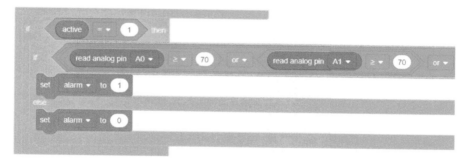

Step 7:

Directly after that we have to define what should happen when the variable "alarm" is activated (i.e. has the value 1). In this case pin 3 should receive current. The piezo buzzer is connected to this pin, which then generates a sound. We use an if-else condition for this!

In this if-else condition, we also nest another if-else condition that is supposed to control our variable "togle", which we already encountered at the very beginning of this project. This variable shall control the alternate blinking of the two red LEDs. These LEDs (pin 8 and pin 9) are supposed to blink when the alarm is triggered, so we switch the variable and the respective pins alternately from 0 to 1 and from 1 to 0, respectively, with an interval of 500 milliseconds (blinking frequency can be changed at will).

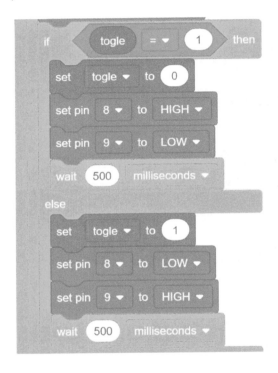

Step 8:

In this last step, we still need to fill in the "else" section of the first if-else condition from step 7. The condition in step 7 was: if "alarm" = 1 then, else. This means that we find the "else" case where the variable "alarm" does not have the value 1 (but has the value 0). In this case, pins 8, 9 and 3 should not receive any current

("LOW"). These are the pins of the piezo buzzer and the two red LEDs, so in this case no alarm and no flashing light should be active.

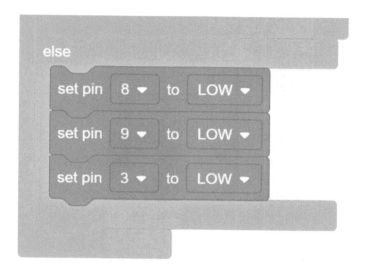

Very good! We made it. Great if you stuck with it. The full illustration of the block code in one piece doesn't make sense here, because you wouldn't be able to see anything due to the size. It makes more sense at this point to have you look at it in Tinkercad if you need to. Use the following link to get to the project: **https://bit.ly/3yqcJCi.**

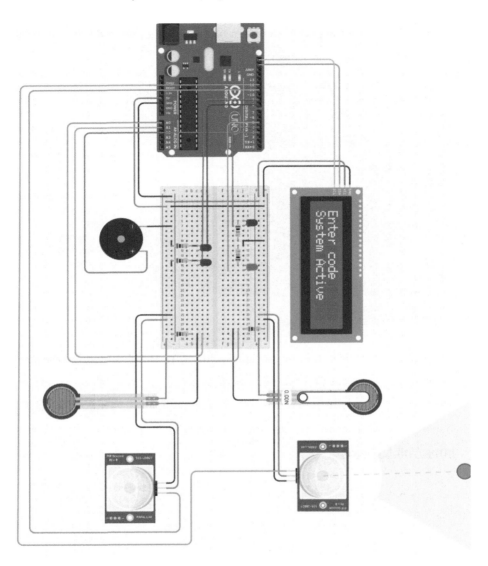

You can set the values of the sensors with one click. With the motion sensor, even a small movement is enough. For the force sensor, you have to set a value of over 0.4 N to trigger an alarm.

At the beginning I mentioned that we will also add a "keypad" here as an alternative to entering the code. But we could do that only in a very complex and tedious way with block code. That's why we'll use text code for this, which I'll show you below.

You can find the Tinkercad project with "Keypad" here: https://bit.ly/3PbxJn2

By the way: We confirm the password entry at the "Keypad" with the "#" key.

The only change we need to make to the schematic is to add the "keypad". We do this by connecting it as shown. The connections on the "Keypad" are for the individual columns and rows (4 + 4 = 8 connections). You can think of the "keypad" as a table.

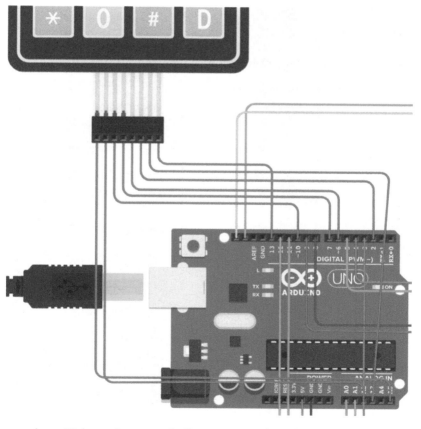

You can have Tinkercad automatically create text-based code from block-based code. This works by switching from Blocks to "Blocks + Text" above the categories

("Output", "Control", "Input", ...) for the block selection. Then the program code will be displayed as text next to the block code.

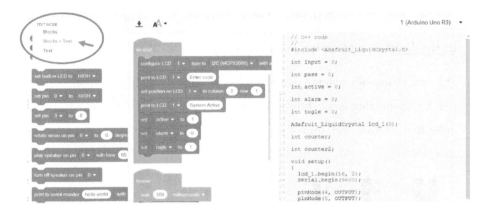

You can now compare the block code with the following text program code that we need for the modified project (incl. "keypad") and thus determine the differences. This is a good exercise to establish a link between block code and text code or to learn the transfer.

The program code is:

```
#include <Adafruit_LiquidCrystal.h>

#include <Keypad.h>


int input = 0;

int pass = 0;

int active = 0;

int alarm = 0;

int togle = 0;

int counter;

int counter2;

const byte ROWS = 4; //four rows

const byte COLS = 4; //four columns
```

```
char keys[ROWS][COLS] = {

  {'1', '2', '3', 'A'},

  {'4', '5', '6', 'B'},

  {'7', '8', '9', 'C'},

  {'*', '0', '#', 'D'}

};

byte rowPins[ROWS] = {A5, A2, 10, 7}; //connect to the row pinouts of the keypad

byte colPins[COLS] = {6, 2, A3, 13}; //connect to the column pinouts of the keypad

String passText = "";

int passLength = 0;


Adafruit_LiquidCrystal lcd_1(0);

Keypad keypad = Keypad( makeKeymap(keys), rowPins, colPins, ROWS, COLS );


void setup()
{
  lcd_1.begin(16, 2);

  Serial.begin(9600);


  pinMode(4, OUTPUT);

  pinMode(5, OUTPUT);

  pinMode(A0, INPUT);

  pinMode(A1, INPUT);

  pinMode(11, INPUT);

  pinMode(12, INPUT);

  pinMode(3, OUTPUT);

  pinMode(8, OUTPUT);

  pinMode(9, OUTPUT);
```

```
  lcd_1.print("Enter code");

  lcd_1.setCursor(0, 1);

  lcd_1.print("System Active");

  active = 1;

  alarm = 0;

  togle = 1;

}


void loop()

{

  //delay(300); // Wait for 300 millisecond(s)

  handle_keypad();

  pass = 0;

  handle_serial_input();


  if (active == 1) {

    if ((analogRead(A0) >= 70 || analogRead(A1) >= 70) || (digitalRead(11) == 1 || digitalRead(12) == 1))
{

      alarm = 1;

    } else {

      alarm = 0;

    }

  }

  if (alarm == 1) {

    digitalWrite(3, HIGH);

    if (togle == 1) {

      togle = 0;

      digitalWrite(8, HIGH);

      digitalWrite(9, LOW);
```

```
      delay(500); // Wait for 500 millisecond(s)
    } else {
      togle = 1;
      digitalWrite(8, LOW);
      digitalWrite(9, HIGH);
      delay(500); // Wait for 500 millisecond(s)
    }
  } else {
    digitalWrite(8, LOW);
    digitalWrite(9, LOW);
    digitalWrite(3, LOW);
  }
}


void active_pass() {
  lcd_1.setCursor(0, 0);
  lcd_1.print("Enter code");
  lcd_1.setCursor(0, 1);
  lcd_1.print("System Active");
  for (counter2 = 0; counter2 < 3; ++counter2) {
    lcd_1.print(" ");
  }
  active = 1;
  digitalWrite(4, LOW);
  digitalWrite(5, HIGH);
}
void wrong_pass() {

  lcd_1.setCursor(0, 0);
```

```
 lcd_1.print("wrong pass");

}

void not_active_pass() {

 lcd_1.setCursor(0, 0);

 lcd_1.print("Enter code");

 lcd_1.setCursor(0, 1);

 lcd_1.print("System not Active");

 active = 0;

 digitalWrite(4, HIGH);

 digitalWrite(5, LOW);

 alarm = 0;


}


void handle_keypad() {

 char key = keypad.getKey();


 if (key) {

  if(passLength == 0){

    lcd_1.setCursor(0, 1);

    lcd_1.print("            ");

    lcd_1.setCursor(0, 1);

   }

  if(key == '#'){

   if(passText == "0378493"){

    active_pass();

    }

    else if(passText == "2047291"){

      not_active_pass();
```

```
        }

    else{

      wrong_pass();

      }

      passText = "";

      passLength = 0;


    return;

    }

  Serial.println(key);

  lcd_1.print(key);

  passText += String(key);

  passLength++;

 }

}


void handle_serial_input(){

  if (Serial.available() > 0) {

   if (Serial.available() == 7) {

    for (counter = 0; counter < 7; ++counter) {

     pass += (pass + Serial.read());

    }

    Serial.println(pass);

    if (pass == 6405 || pass == 6371) {

     if (pass == 6405) {

      active_pass();


     }

     if (pass == 6371) {
```

```
        not_active_pass();

     }

   } else {

     wrong_pass();

   }

  } else {

    wrong_pass();

  }

  input = Serial.read();

 }

 }
```

6 Project 3 | Plant monitoring

This project is for all those who unfortunately too often forget to water and care for their plants. In this project we will monitor a plant with the help of sensors and intervene with actuators in case of deviations.

As sensors we use a soil moisture sensor, which can be placed in a flowerpot. This monitors the moisture of the plant soil. We also use an ambient light sensor that detects the ambient light near the plant. And finally, we also use a temperature sensor that monitors the ambient temperature near the plant.

The temperature, the brightness of the ambient light and the humidity of the plant soil are to be displayed to us for control with the help of three "7-Segment Clock Displays". Displaying is to take place in percent, thus from 0 - 100. The value 0 shall mean that the temperature is the lowest, the ambient light is the weakest, and the plant soil is very dry. The value 100, on the other hand, shall mean that the temperature is the highest, the ambient light is the strongest and the plant soil is very moist. One "7-segment clock display" is provided per sensor.

So that the plant is also supplied when we are not at home, we would also like to install a few actuators. So that the plant gets water, we have a servo motor controlled, which could then open a water access via a mechanism, for example. We also want two light bulbs to be turned on when the temperature drops below 15° C, and turned off again when the temperature reaches at least 15° C. We use an incandescent lamp here as a temporary electric heater, since it radiates a lot of heat as well as light. At dusk (ambient light sensor), the plant should also be illuminated with red light for 15 seconds (15 minutes would be better, but that would be too long for our simulation purposes), which should improve the plant's sleep phase. For this purpose, we use three RGB LEDs.

6.1 Required components

Link to the Tinkercad project: https://bit.ly/3bYWogc

Quantity	Designation
1	Arduino Uno
1	Breadboard (small)
1	Ambient light sensor
1	Temperature sensor TMP36
1	Soil moisture sensor
2	Light bulb
3	RGB LEDs
1	100 kΩ resistor for ambient light sensor
1	20 Ω resistor for RGB LEDs
1	Servo motor
3	7-Segment Clock Display

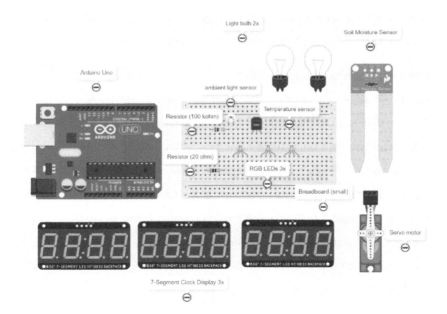

Refresher for the TMP36 temperature sensor:

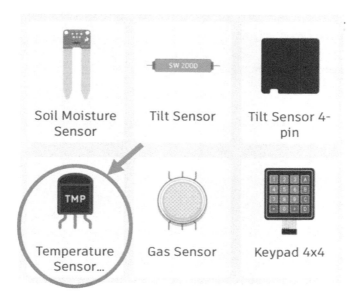

We had already used the TMP36 once in the first book of the series. Here is a brief refresher on how to use it.

The TMP36 is a low-voltage temperature sensor. The special feature of this temperature sensor is its linearity over the entire temperature measuring range. The sensor has three connections: "+VS", "GND" and "Vout". The "Vout" pin of this sensor provides an output voltage that is linearly proportional to the measured temperature in degrees Celsius. The operating voltage of the sensor is 5V DC, which allows it to be used directly with an Arduino UNO. For every one degree Celsius change in temperature, the output voltage changes by 10 millivolts. At 25 °C, the output voltage is 750 mV. A full datasheet can be downloaded from the following link:

https://www.analog.com/media/en/technical-documentation/data-sheets/TMP35_36_37.pdf

At 0 degrees Celsius, the quantized analog voltage value is equal to 104. On this basis, we can perform the required conversion from sensor value to temperature as follows:

Temp_C = (sensor value - 104) * 165/338.

6.2 The design of the circuit diagram

Before we start wiring our components, let's first look again at the schematic view of the required circuit diagram.

Schematic circuit diagram:

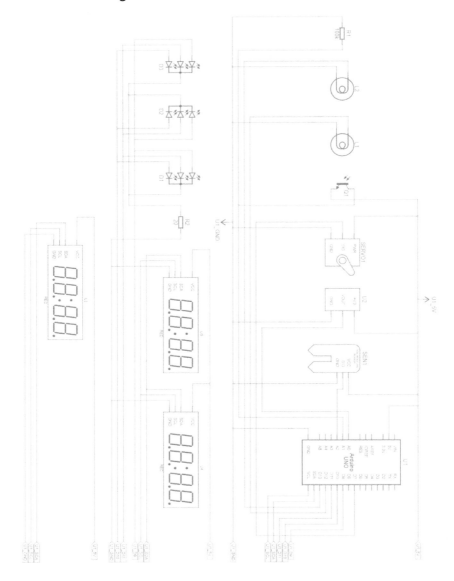

We start for the wiring as usual with the breadboard as starting point in the middle of the circuit and the Arduino to the left.

We equip the breadboard with the ambient light sensor, the temperature sensor and the three RGB LEDs. In addition, we also attach the two resistors at the position shown. After that we supply the breadboard with power. To do this, we connect a red and a black wire from the Arduino (5V and GND pins, respectively) to the two supply connectors ("+" and "-") of the breadboard in the lower area. Furthermore, we link the lower area with the upper area.

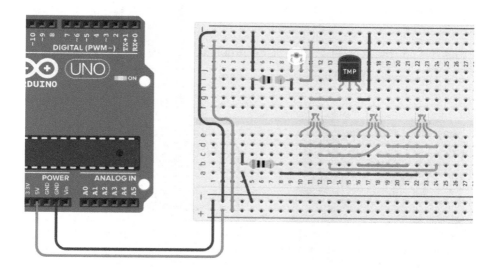

For the RGB LEDs we connect the connections for the colors (red, blue, green) with each other and connect the cathode (black) via the 20 Ω resistor. The temperature sensor is supplied with current (red and black) and the ambient light sensor is also supplied with current via the 100 kΩ resistor. If you are now wondering which connections of the temperature sensor and the RGB LEDs stand for which function, take a look at the following figure to refresh your knowledge:

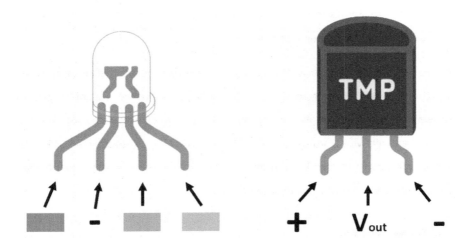

Then we link the RGB LEDs to the digital Arduino pins 9, 10 and 11 via a red, a blue and a green wire so that we can control them.

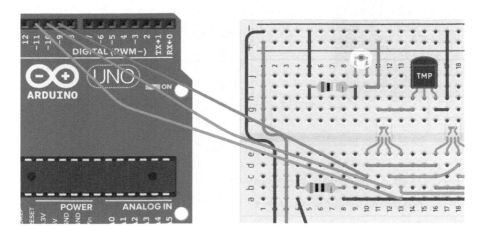

Next, we take care of the ambient light sensor and the temperature sensor. We connect the ambient light sensor with a light blue wire via the resistor at pin "C" to the analog input A1 of the Arduino. We connect the temperature sensor to the analog input A0 of the Arduino with a yellow wire via the middle pin (V_{out}).

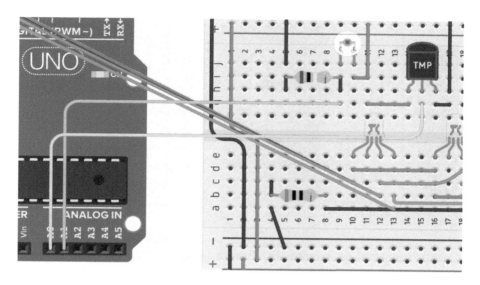

We continue with the light bulbs, which we connect on the one hand to the power supply of our breadboard ("-") and on the other hand to the digital pins 12 and 13 of the Arduino.

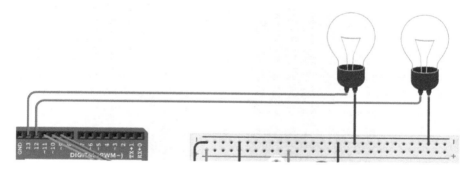

Now we have almost made it! Only the soil moisture sensor, the servo motor and the three displays are missing. First, we connect the soil moisture sensor. The pinout for it is printed on the sensor. There are the connections VCC ("+"), GND ("-") and SIG (signal). So we have to power the sensor again first, for this we connect it to the breadboard. Then we connect the SIG connector to the analog input A2 of the Arduino.

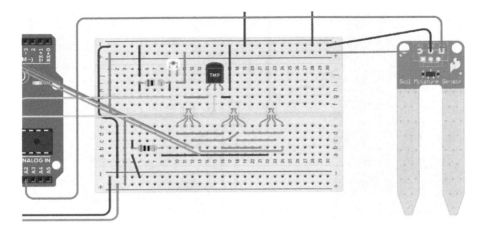

We also supply the servo motor with voltage as usual (left pin: " - ", middle pin: " + "). And we supply the connection for the control signal (right pin) via the digital pin 7 of the Arduino.

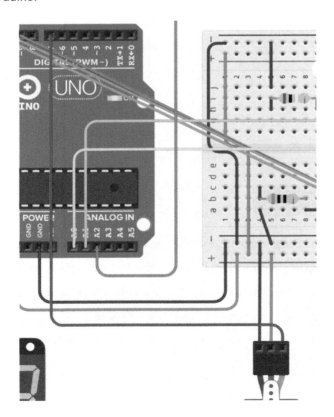

Finally, we have to connect the "7-Segment Clock Displays". The "0.56 inch 7-Segment LED HT16K33 Backpack Displays" used here have four connectors. Two of them are for power supply (printed "+" and "-") and two of them are for signal control (printed "C" and "D"). The addition of "HT16K33 Backpack" means that the displays each have a "HT16K33 I2C LED Driver" installed, which - as with the I2C LCD display - allows control via the SDA and SLC connectors of the Arduino.

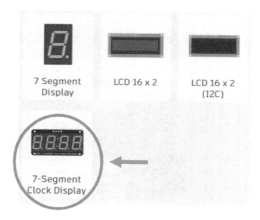

Via breadboard and Arduino, we first supply the displays with power.

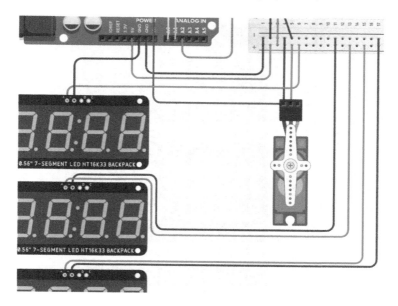

Then we put the signal lines in turquoise (pin "C" of the respective display to pin "SCL" of the Arduino) and brown (pin "D" of the respective display to pin "SDA" of the Arduino).

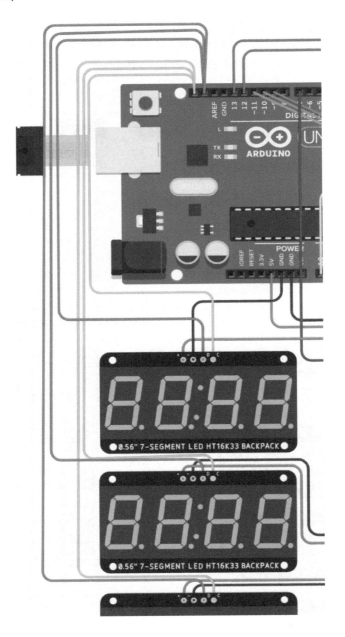

Complete circuit diagram:

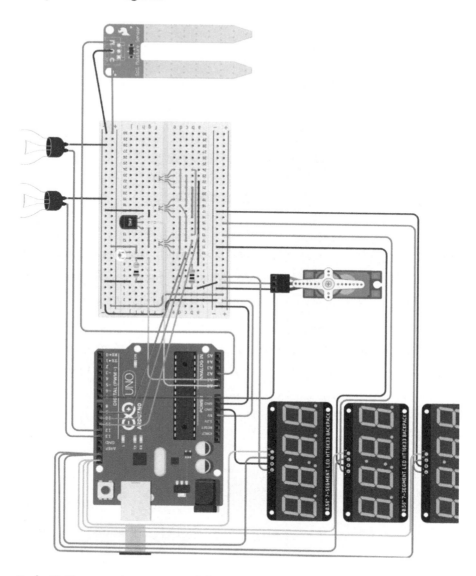

Perfect! Now we have successfully connected all components and can start programming! Let's go!

6.3 Development of the program code

In this chapter we will go step by step through the required programming. The programming will be a bit shorter and easier than in the previous project.

Step 1:

In the first step we start - as usual - with the optional title block (to be found in the category "Notation") and the text "plant monitoring".

Step 2:

In the second step, we add the "on start" block, which executes a certain line of code only once when the program starts. What code do we need to execute only once in this project? Think about the other two projects! We don't have **LCD** displays here, but we need to configure the 7-segment **LED** displays as well. We do that with the command "configure LED display ..." from the category "Output". We can see the number and address by clicking on the respective display. In the settings menu that opens, you can also change the color of the light.

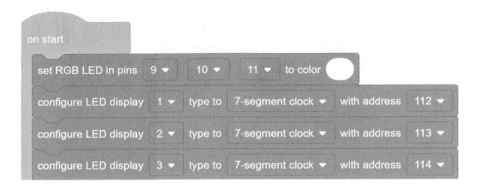

We also set the variable "timeCounter", which we will need later for the RGB LEDs, to the initial value 0.

In order to do that, we have to create the variable in the category "Variables" by clicking on "Create Variable ...". We also create all the other required variables at the same time. In this project we still need the variables "light" for the ambient light, "soil" for the soil moisture and "temp" for the ambient temperature.

The "on start" command is now finished, and the variables are created. So now we can move on to the next step.

Step 3:

In this step we start with the code for the "forever" block. First, we want to read the sensor values and display them on the LED displays. To do this, we first read the sensor values, scale them each with a factor for better display and then assign the value to the respective variable.

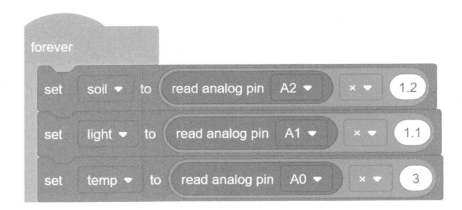

To show us the values in percent between 0 and 100 on the display, we use on the one hand the already known function "map ()" (to convert the sensor values) and on the other hand the function "constrain ()" to limit the temperature value to a range from 0 to 100. The detailed documentation for the function "constrain ()" can be found here:

https://www.arduino.cc/reference/en/language/functions/math/constrain/

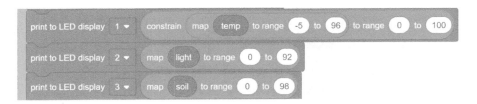

With "print to LED display ..." we can then display the respective sensor value converted into the range of 0 - 100 on the respective display.

Step 4:

Now we only need the control of the actuators, i.e. the control of the servo motor that will regulate the water supply, the control of the RGB LEDs and the control of the bulbs based on the ambient light as well as the ambient temperature.

We start in this step with the control of the RGB LEDs. We want the LEDs to light up in red for 15 seconds as soon as it gets dark. For this we first use an if-condition and implement the following statement: If the value of the variable "light" (sensor value ambient light sensor) is smaller than the value 500 (can also be changed; just try it out), then we should wait 1 second and then increase the value of the variable "timeCounter" by +1.

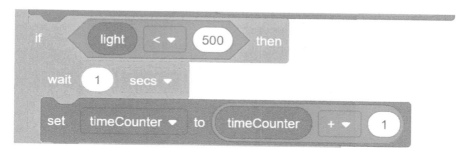

Our RGB LEDs should light up for 15 seconds, i.e. we now need an if-else condition that says the following: If the variable "timeCounter" is less than 15 (value 15 stands for 15 seconds here, because we waited 1 second each time before increasing the value of the variable), then the LED should light up in red, otherwise the LED should be off. Try it yourself before you take a look at the following figure (solution)!

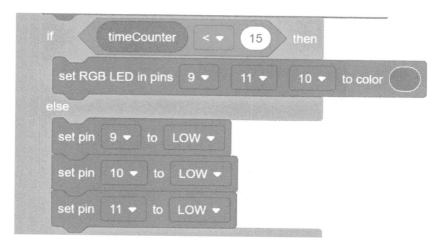

As you can see, there is a separate command to determine the color of the RGB LEDs. All we have to do here is select the Arduino pins to which the LEDs are connected (9, 10, 11) and then we can determine the color. If we don't want the LED to light up, we simply set the connection pins to "LOW" ("off").

Step 5:

In this step we continue with the control of the servo motor, which could regulate a water supply. From a certain moisture of the plant soil (=value of the soil moisture sensor) the water supply should either be opened or stopped. We use an if-else condition for this and determine that the sensor value must be either smaller or larger than 500 (freely selected) so that the water supply is activated or deactivated.

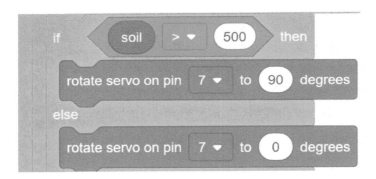

As we can see, in this program code we have assumed that the water supply is open when the servo motor is at the 0 degrees position. The water supply is closed when the servo motor moves to the 90 degrees position. This is the case when there is enough moisture in the soil (sensor value stored in "soil" is greater than 500). We could have written this code in a different way. Do you know how? For example, we could have written that the water supply should open (0-degree position or also 90-degree position; depending on when the water supply is open) when the value of "soil" is less than 500 (so the potting soil is too dry). One comes with it on the same action.

Step 6:

Almost identically to step 5, we also proceed in this step for the control of the two bulbs based on the ambient temperature. You are welcome to try it on your own first, that's how you learn best! Pause here for a moment and then look at the solution.

We want the light bulbs (our temporary heater) to light up when it gets too cold (temperature value below 15° C). We use an if-else condition for this. The equation for the temperature value is: Temp_C = (sensor value - 104) * 165/338. We also multiplied our variable "temp" by a factor of 3 at the beginning, so we have to take that into account here, too. So, in order to find out the value we have to specify for 15 °C in our condition, we have to calculate as follows: temp = ((Temp_C * 338/165) + 104) *3. So: temp = ((15 °C * 338/165) + 104) * 3 = 404.18. We round the value to 400, which is the value we need to specify for the variable "temp" in the if-else condition.

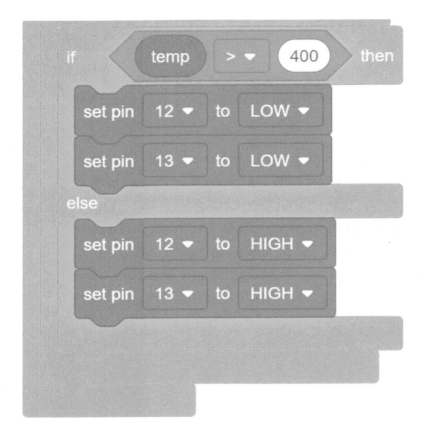

So here we have implemented the following: If the temperature is greater than 15 °C (temp > 400), then pins 12 and 13, which control the circuit of the two bulbs, should receive the value "LOW" ("off"). Otherwise (i.e. when the temperature falls below 15 °C or the sensor value 400), the bulbs should receive current so that they can light up (pins 12 and 13 "HIGH").

Great job! Now we are done with the program code and can enjoy the simulation. The values for the sensors can be simulated - as usual - with the help of a slider when you click on the respective sensor. By the way, the LEDS already light up for 15 seconds at the beginning, because the output value of the sensor is set to completely dark due to the program. The servo motor also moves briefly to 90° and back for initialization.

```
title block comment ( plant monitoring )

on start
  configure LED display  1 ▾  type to  7-segment clock ▾  with address  112 ▾
  configure LED display  2 ▾  type to  7-segment clock ▾  with address  113 ▾
  configure LED display  3 ▾  type to  7-segment clock ▾  with address  114 ▾
  set  timeCounter ▾  to  0

forever
  set  soil ▾  to  ( read analog pin  A2 ▾  x ▾  1.2 )
  set  light ▾  to  ( read analog pin  A1 ▾  x ▾  1.1 )
  set  temp ▾  to  ( read analog pin  A0 ▾  x ▾  3 )
  print to LED display  1 ▾  ( constrain  map  temp  to range  -5  to  96  to range  0  to  100 )
  print to LED display  2 ▾  ( map  light  to range  0  to  92 )
  print to LED display  3 ▾  ( map  soil  to range  0  to  98 )
  if  ( light  < ▾  500 )  then
    wait  1  secs ▾
    set  timeCounter ▾  to  ( timeCounter  + ▾  1 )
    if  ( timeCounter  < ▾  15 )  then
      set RGB LED in pins  9 ▾  11 ▾  10 ▾  to color  (  )
    else
      set pin  9 ▾  to  LOW ▾
      set pin  10 ▾  to  LOW ▾
      set pin  11 ▾  to  LOW ▾

    if  ( soil  > ▾  500 )  then
      rotate servo on pin  7 ▾  to  90  degrees
    else
      rotate servo on pin  7 ▾  to  0  degrees

    if  ( temp  > ▾  400 )  then
      set pin  12 ▾  to  LOW ▾
      set pin  13 ▾  to  LOW ▾
    else
      set pin  12 ▾  to  HIGH ▾
      set pin  13 ▾  to  HIGH ▾
```

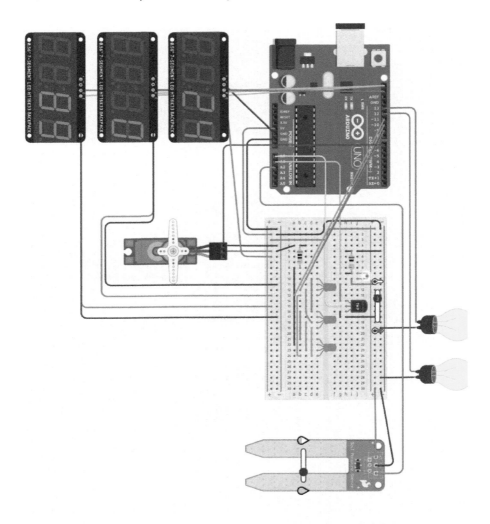

You can set the values of the sensors again by clicking on them and using the slider.

7 Project 4 | Parking assistance and garage air monitoring

In this project we dedicate ourselves to a parking aid for our car in the garage. The system can be attached to the garage wall, for example, and should show us how much distance we have to the wall with our car.

In this project we use an ultrasonic sensor to determine the distance and an LCD display to show the distance. The distance between the sensor and the object (e.g. the bumper of the car), should be shown on the display in "cm". The process should start at a distance of about 320 cm (maximum distance the ultrasonic sensor can measure) and end at a distance of about 2 cm (minimum distance the ultrasonic sensor can measure).

To make this project a bit more complicated, we will also monitor the garage door. For example, we can put a tilt sensor on the garage door. When the garage door is closed (tilt door), an RGB LED should light up in yellow, for example. As soon as the garage door is fully closed, the RGB LED should light up in green, for example. The monitoring for the complete closing could be done e.g. by a force sensor - at the stop point of the garage door.

Finally, we will integrate a gas sensor into the project to monitor the garage air. As soon as a significant amount of gas is detected, a red LED flashes and a buzzer sounds. In addition, in this case a servo motor should move to the 90° position, which could, for example, open a window for fresh air supply via a mechanism. As soon as no more gas is detected, the process should run backwards, i.e. the motor should close the window by moving to the 0° position. The LED and the sound should then also be switched off.

7.1 Required components

Link to the Tinkercad project: https://bit.ly/3aj86Sv

Quantity	Designation
1	Arduino Uno
1	Breadboard (small)
1	ultrasonic sensor **Parallax PING)))**
1	Tilt sensor SW 200D
1	Force sensor
1	Gas sensor
1	Servo motor
1	Piezo buzzer
1	RGB LEDs
1	LED (red)
1	10 kΩ resistor for tilt sensor
2	100 Ω resistor for RGB LED and LED
2	1 kΩ resistor for gas sensor and force sensor
1	LCD display 16×2 **(I2C and MCP23008 based)**

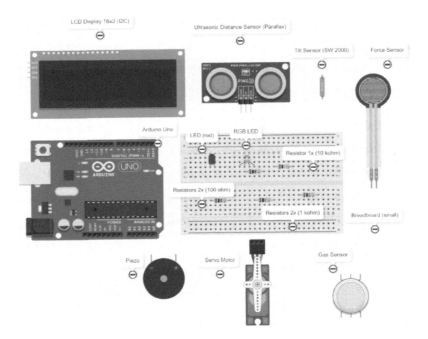

Refresh to the "Parallax PING 28015" ultrasonic sensor:

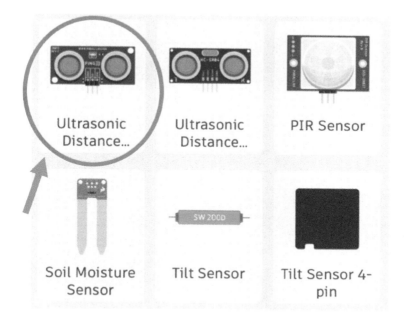

The "PING 28015" sensor from "Parallax" is a low-cost proximity sensor based on ultrasound. According to the manufacturer's data sheet, the detection range of this sensor is between 2 cm and 300 cm, which can be considered a good range. A special feature of this sensor is that it can communicate with a microcontroller, e.g. the Arduino, using only a single pin ("SIG"). On the one hand this makes the connection so easy, on the other hand it helps in complex projects to be able to use the limited number of input and output pins with many other components. The sensor has two additional connections "GND" and "5V", which, as you can probably guess by now, are necessary for the power supply. You can download the complete datasheet e.g. here: https://www.mouser.com/datasheet/2/321/28015-PING-Sensor-Product-Guide-v2.0-461050.pdf

7.2 The design of the circuit diagram

Before we start wiring our components, let's first look again at the schematic view of the required circuit diagram.

Schematic circuit diagram:

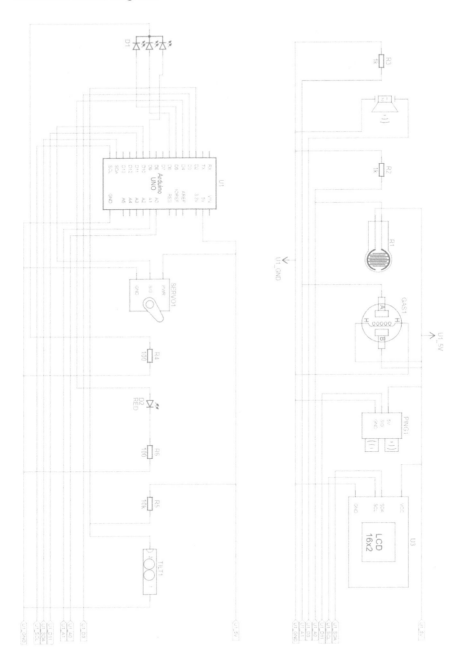

We start for the wiring as usual with the breadboard as starting point in the middle of the circuit and the Arduino to the left.

We equip the breadboard with the red LED, the RGB LED and the resistors as shown. Then we connect the breadboard with the power supply of the Arduino (5V and GND at the Arduino and "+" and "-" at the breadboard). We also connect the top two "+" and "-" lines of the breadboard to the power supply. Finally we add black and red lines as shown. We will need these for the other components.

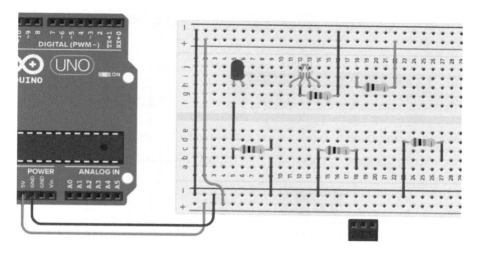

Then we connect the pins of the RGB LED (blue, green, red) to the Arduino pins 5, 6 and 9. Furthermore we connect the anode of the red LED to the Arduino pin 4.

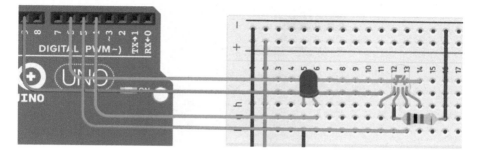

Then we connect the LCD display. We already have practice in this.

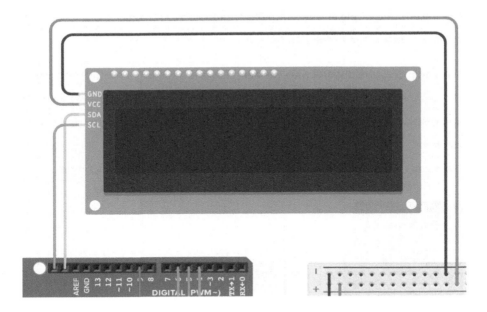

We also wire the piezo buzzer, using Arduino pin 3 on one side (yellow wire) and connecting the piezo to the ground ("-") of the breadboard on the other side.

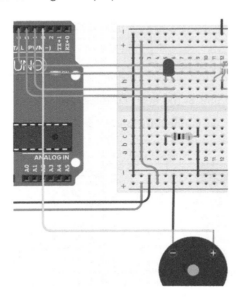

We then also connect the servo motor by supplying power to it and by placing a purple wire from Arduino pin 10 to the servo motor's signal jack.

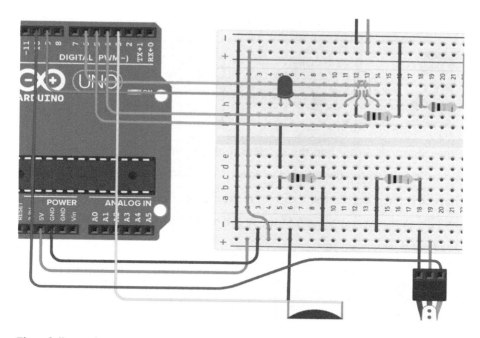

Then follows the connection of the ultrasonic sensor. Here we also need a power supply and in addition we lay a data line (orange) from "SIG" to Arduino pin 11.

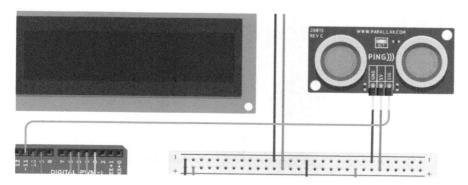

Now we can also connect the tilt sensor. For this we connect one connector of the sensor (which one doesn't matter) to the "-" line of the breadboard. The other connection we divide over a yellow line. On the one hand we supply the sensor via a resistor with the "+" line of the breadboard, on the other hand we connect a pink data line to Arduino pin 2, so that we can read out the value of the sensor later.

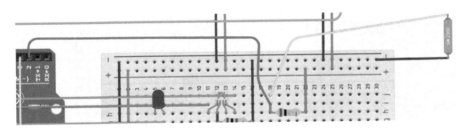

Now the force sensor and the gas sensor are missing, which we connect to the power supply of the breadboard as follows (red and black lines). In addition, we have to connect one data line each from the sensors (light blue for the force sensor and green for the gas sensor) to the Arduino pins A0 and A1, so that we can also read out their values later.

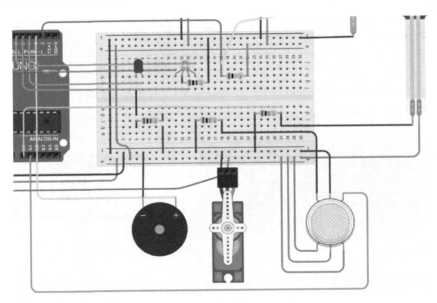

Complete circuit diagram:

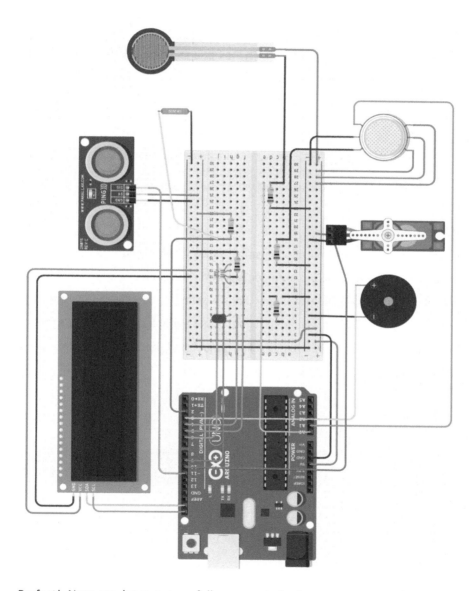

Perfect! Now we have successfully connected all components and can start programming! Let's go!

7.3 Development of the program code

In this chapter we will again go step by step through the required programming.

Step 1:

In the first step we start - as usual - with the optional title block (to be found in the "Notation" category) and the description: "parking assistance and garage-air monitoring".

Step 2:

In the second step, we add the "on start" block, which executes a certain line of code only once when the program starts. What code do we need to execute only once in this project? By now we know that we definitely need to configure the LCD display. Also, we assign a value of 0 to one of our variables (we have yet to create it) at the beginning. The variable is called "togle" and should later be responsible for the blinking of the red LED (similar to project 2).

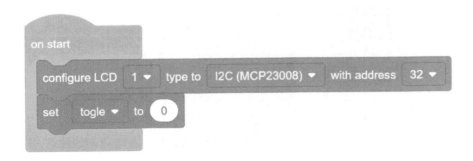

Step 3:

Now we also create all the other required variables. These are: "distance" for the distance sensor, "tilt" for the tilt sensor, "force" for the force sensor and "gas" for the gas sensor.

Step 4:

Now we use the previously created variables to store the respective sensor values - after reading them out - in them. We do this - as we are used to by now - with? Exactly, with "set ... to" and "read ...".

There is a special feature to note with the ultrasonic sensor. Our ultrasonic sensor has connections for the power supply (5V and GND) and a connection for the signal (SIG). This connection is also called "trigger" for other sensors. When this pin of the sensor receives a signal, the ultrasonic sensor emits an ultrasonic wave. In other sensors, however, there is an additional pin called "Echo" where a signal is present as soon as the ultrasonic signal reflected back from the object has been received again by the sensor. This is the case, for example, with the "HC-SR04" ultrasonic sensor:

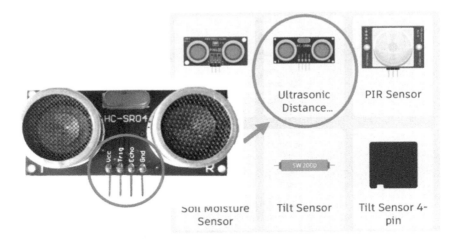

In our case, however, the sensor has only one pin (SIG) for these two functions, so we set the trigger pin to 11 (connection on the Arduino) and the "echo pin" to "same as trigger". In addition, we specify the unit of measurement in which the measured value is to be output (cm).

The other sensors are read out normally either with "read digital ..." or "read analog ..." at their connection pins (2, A0, A1) and the measured values are then stored in the respective variable with "set ...".

Step 5:

Since we want to display the value measured by the ultrasonic sensor on the LCD display, we will create the programming for this in this step. Consider if you might already be able to do this on your own. It is relatively simple, we will use the same commands that we always use when we want to show something on a display. Display: "Distance: *value* cm"

Here's how we can make that happen:

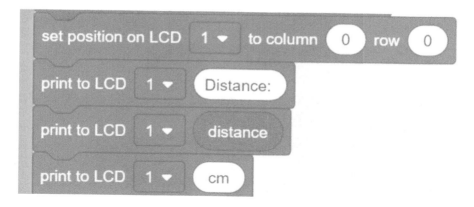

Step 6:

Next, we implement the warning function (piezo sound and flashing of the red LED) and the mechanism for opening the window (servo motor). You are also welcome to try this on your own first! We set the threshold value for activation to 110 (gas sensor), for example. You can also program the blinking process of the LED at the same time, we had already implemented such a process in project 2.

Help: First use an if-else condition (If "gas" > value, then action ... otherwise action backwards) and in this first if-else condition use another nested if-else condition for the blinking. Use the variable "togle" and the two values "0" or "1" for the blinking process.

Solution:

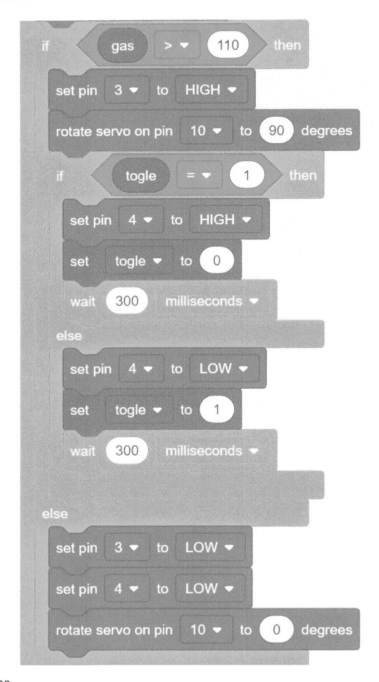

It may be that your solution looks structurally a bit different, as long as the content is identical and the function is guaranteed, the solution can also look different, here there is not only one way. Just try your solution and see if it works.

Step 7:

The actions for the force sensor and the tilt sensor are still missing. In this step, we will first deal with the force sensor. If the force is greater than the threshold value 70, the RGB LED should light up in green, because the garage door is then closed. We can implement this quite simply as follows:

Step 8:

In this last step we also implement the tilt sensor. The RGB LED should light up yellow as soon as the garage door tilts, otherwise the RGB LED should light up white. The tilt sensor delivers the digital signal "ON" ("1") when it is in horizontal position (no tilt). As soon as the tilt sensor is held at an angle (>10 degrees; tilting), a small ball inside rolls to the other end. This breaks the circuit, and the sensor delivers the signal "OFF" ("0"). So basically, the sensor is just a tilt-sensitive switch.

So we need to create a program code that makes the RGB shine in yellow when the sensor returns the value "0" (use variable "tilt"). Otherwise, the RGB should shine in white. Try it out! The solution follows shortly.

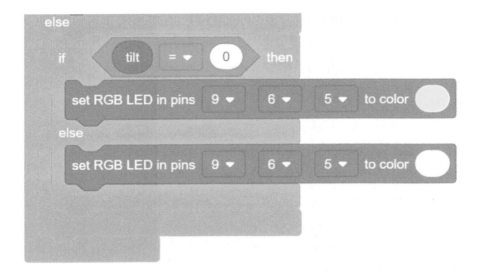

Perfect! Now we have also successfully completed this project and can start the simulation in Tinkercad.

After that we will continue with our last project! Soon we'll have it done. In the meantime, you can probably already independently implement a few more projects that you may have wanted to do for a long time.

title block comment (parking assistance and garage-air monitoring)

on start

configure LCD 1 ▾ type to I2C (MCP23008) ▾ with address 32 ▾

set togle ▾ to 0

forever

set distance ▾ to read ultrasonic distance sensor on trigger pin 11 ▾ echo pin same as trigger ▾ in units cm ▾

set tilt ▾ to read digital pin 2 ▾

set force ▾ to read analog pin A0 ▾

set gas ▾ to read analog pin A1 ▾

set position on LCD 1 ▾ to column 0 row 0

print to LCD 1 ▾ (Distance:)

print to LCD 1 ▾ distance

print to LCD 1 ▾ (cm)

if (gas > ▾ 110) then

set pin 3 ▾ to HIGH ▾

rotate servo on pin 10 ▾ to 90 degrees

if (togle = ▾ 1) then

set pin 4 ▾ to HIGH ▾

set togle ▾ to 0

wait 300 milliseconds ▾

else

set pin 4 ▾ to LOW ▾

set togle ▾ to 1

wait 300 milliseconds ▾

else

set pin 3 ▾ to LOW ▾

set pin 4 ▾ to LOW ▾

rotate servo on pin 10 ▾ to 0 degrees

if (force > ▾ 70) then

set RGB LED in pins 9 ▾ 6 ▾ 5 ▾ to color

else

if (tilt = ▾ 0) then

set RGB LED in pins 9 ▾ 6 ▾ 5 ▾ to color

else

set RGB LED in pins 9 ▾ 6 ▾ 5 ▾ to color

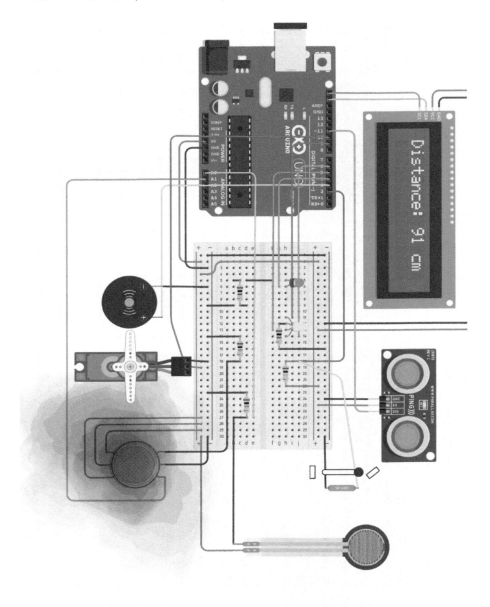

In this project, we have displayed the distance in "cm" on the LCD display. You could also display the distance with a NeoPixel ring (24 LEDs).

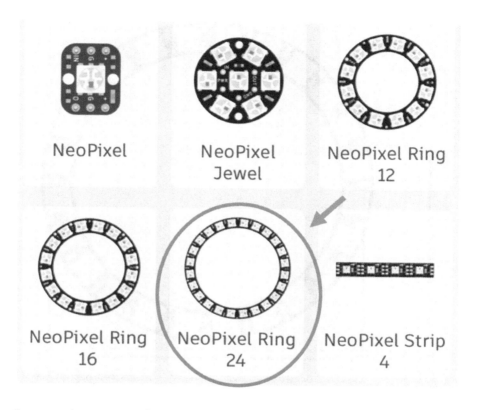

For example, we want all LEDs of the ring to light up as soon as we are very close to the garage wall with the car. The further away we are, the fewer LEDs of the ring should light up. If we are very far away, no LED should light up at all.

You can find the Tinkercad project with Neopixel LED here: https://bit.ly/3P8RBaC

In the circuit diagram of the original project, we need to make the following two changes:

1. We delete the LCD display and its wiring

2. We wire the NeoPixel LED ring (24) as follows (red, black, green):

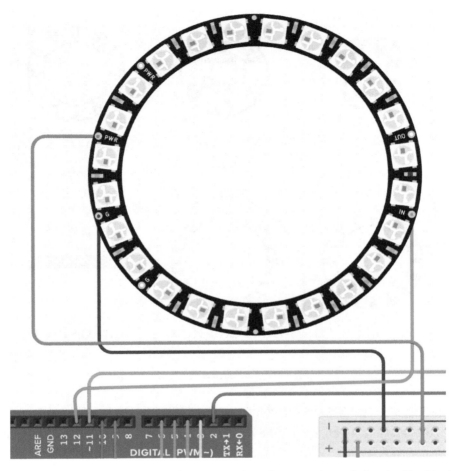

For programming, however, we have to work with text code again for the NeoPixel ring, since no block is available for this component. You can switch back to the "Block+Text" display in Tinkercad for the original project and in this way compare the code with the following text code.

The program code is:

#include <Adafruit_NeoPixel.h>

#include <Servo.h>

```
int distance = 0;

int telt = 0;

int force = 0;

int gas = 0;

int togle = 0;

#define PIN 12


Servo servo_10;

Adafruit_NeoPixel strip = Adafruit_NeoPixel(24, PIN, NEO_GRB + NEO_KHZ800);


long readUltrasonicDistance(int triggerPin, int echoPin)

{

  pinMode(triggerPin, OUTPUT);  // Clear the trigger

  digitalWrite(triggerPin, LOW);

  delayMicroseconds(2);

  // Sets the trigger pin to HIGH state for 10 microseconds

  digitalWrite(triggerPin, HIGH);

  delayMicroseconds(10);

  digitalWrite(triggerPin, LOW);

  pinMode(echoPin, INPUT);

  // Reads the echo pin, and returns the sound wave travel time in microseconds

  return pulseIn(echoPin, HIGH);

}
```

```
void setup()

{

  pinMode(2, INPUT);

  pinMode(A0, INPUT);

  pinMode(A1, INPUT);

  pinMode(9, OUTPUT);

  pinMode(6, OUTPUT);

  pinMode(5, OUTPUT);

  pinMode(3, OUTPUT);

  servo_10.attach(10, 500, 2500);

  strip.begin();

  pinMode(4, OUTPUT);

Serial.begin(9600);

  togle = 0;

}


void loop()

{

  distance = 0.01723 * readUltrasonicDistance(11, 11);

  telt = digitalRead(2);

  force = analogRead(A0);

  gas = analogRead(A1);

  Serial.println(distance);

  LedStrip();
```

98

```
if (gas > 110) {

  digitalWrite(3, HIGH);

  servo_10.write(90);

  if (togle == 1) {

   digitalWrite(4, HIGH);

   togle = 0;

   delay(300); // Wait for 300 millisecond(s)

  } else {

   digitalWrite(4, LOW);

   togle = 1;

   delay(300); // Wait for 300 millisecond(s)

  }

 } else {

  digitalWrite(3, LOW);

  digitalWrite(4, LOW);

  servo_10.write(0);

 }

if (force > 70) {

 analogWrite(9, 51);

 analogWrite(6, 255);

 analogWrite(5, 51);

} else {

 if (telt == 0) {

  analogWrite(9, 255);
```

```
    analogWrite(6, 255);

    analogWrite(5, 0);

  } else {

    analogWrite(9, 255);

    analogWrite(6, 255);

    analogWrite(5, 255);

  }

 }

}

void LedStrip()

{

 int level = map(distance, 20, 300, 24, 0);

 for(byte i=0; i<level; i++)

 {

  strip.setPixelColor(i, 0, 0, 255);

 }

 for(byte i=level; i<24; i++)

 {

  strip.setPixelColor(i, 0, 0, 0);

 }

 strip.show();

}
```

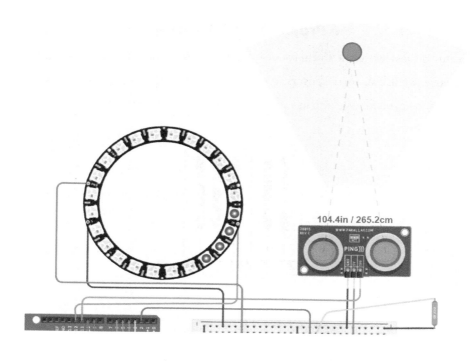

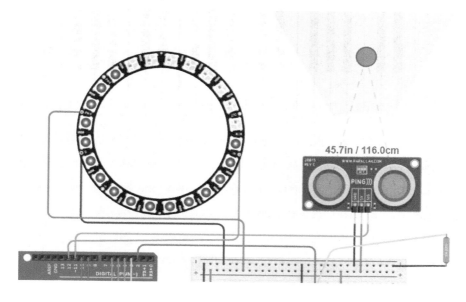

8 Project 5 | Mini Piano

In this project we want to reproduce a few keys of a piano keyboard. For this purpose, we use six force sensors to represent the keys C4, D4, E4, F4, G4 and A4 of a piano keyboard. We also use six piezo buzzers, each responsible for one of the keys.

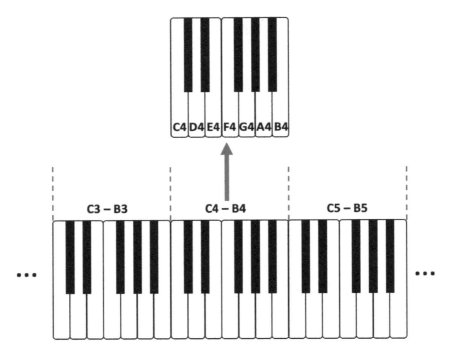

Depending on which key is pressed, the corresponding sound should be generated. This should also work if you press several keys at the same time. Therefore, we use a piezo buzzer for each key in this project. For each tone we have to drive the corresponding piezo buzzer with a different frequency. For example, tone A4, also known as a tuning tone or chamber tone, has a frequency of 440 Hz, while tone C4 has about 262 Hz. In the following table, the frequencies are assigned to the respective tones. In block programming in Tinkercad, we also need a specific code for the respective tone. These are also listed in the table. In text-based programming, by the way, we could just use the normal frequency.

Sound	Frequency [Hz]	Tinkercad Code
C4	262	48
D4	294	50
E4	330	52
F4	349	53
G4	392	55
A4	440	57

When a "key" is pressed (i.e. the force sensor measures a force), the corresponding LED of the key should also light up and remain lit until the key is released again.

8.1 Required components

Link to the Tinkercad project: https://bit.ly/3apcY8D

Quantity	Designation
1	Arduino Uno
1	Breadboard (small)
6	Piezo buzzer
6	Force sensor
6	LED (blue)
6	1 kΩ resistor for force sensors
6	1 kΩ resistor for LEDs

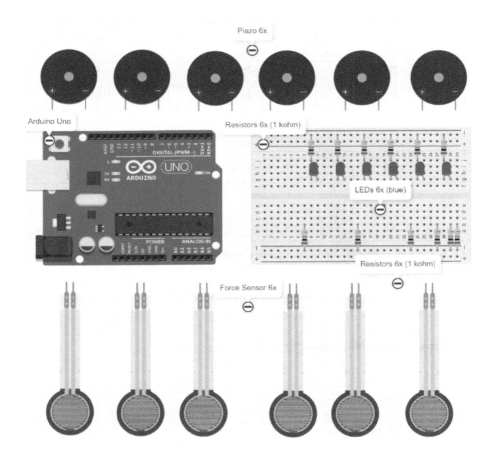

8.2 The design of the circuit diagram

Before we start wiring our components, let's first look again at the schematic view of the required circuit diagram.

Schematic circuit diagram:

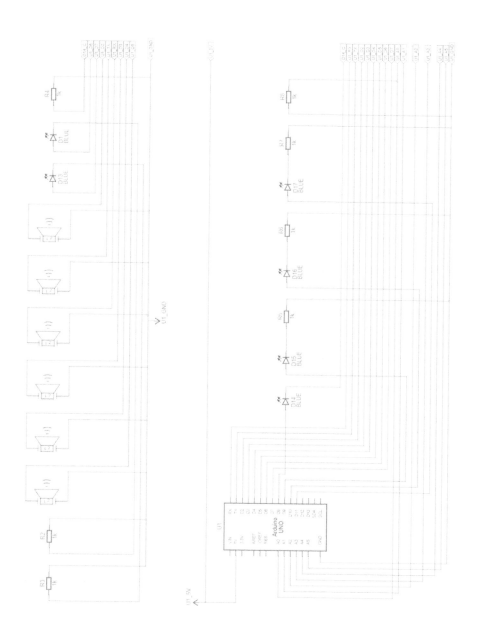

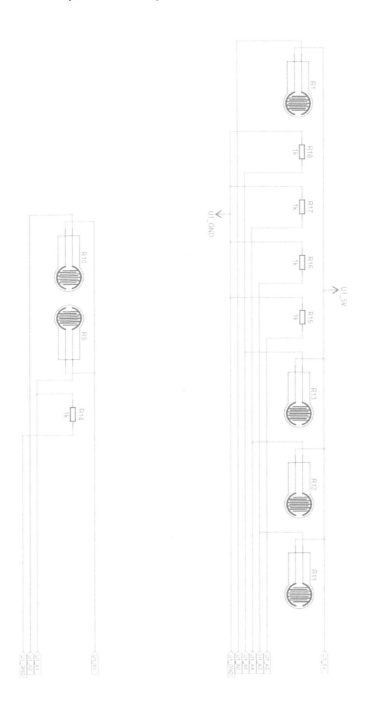

We start for the wiring as usual with the breadboard as starting point in the middle of the circuit and the Arduino to the left. We equip our breadboard with the LEDs and the resistors as shown. We also supply power to the breadboard via the Arduino ("GND" and "5V"). We also connect again, as usual, the upper and lower power supply lines of the breadboard. Finally, we add a few very short black wires, which will serve us later for the further connection of the components.

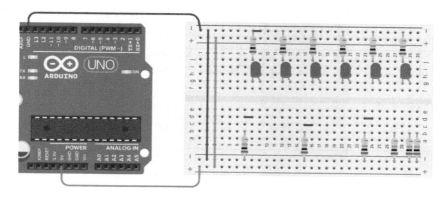

Next we want to connect the LEDs. Since they already have a connection from the cathode to "-" through the resistors, we only need a connection from the anode to the Arduino board. It's best to try it yourself first before continuing here (Arduino pins 6, 7, 8, 9, 10, 11).

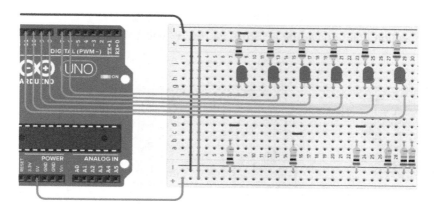

Then we take care of the connection of the force sensors. First we connect a red and a black wire from the force sensors to the breadboard to ensure the power supply of the sensors.

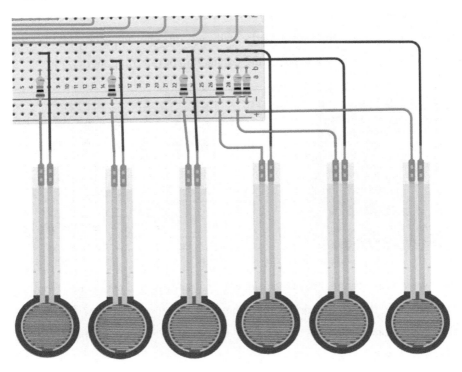

Now we still need the data lines (green), which we connect from the force sensors (connection point above the resistors via the "+" lines) to the analog inputs A0 - A5.

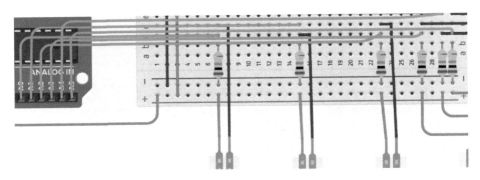

The last thing we have to do is to connect our piezo buzzers. First we connect black wires from the "-" pole of the piezo buzzer to the "-" supply line of the breadboard.

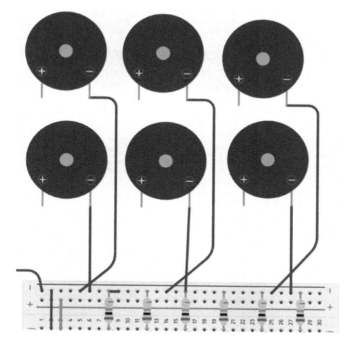

To be able to control the piezo buzzers, we connect orange lines from the "+" pole of the piezo buzzers to the digital pins 0, 1, 2, 3, 4 and 5.

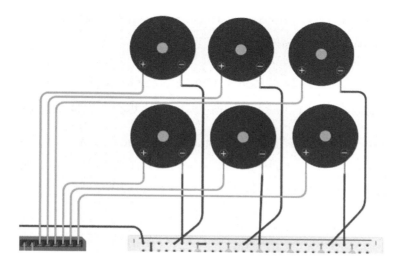

Complete circuit diagram:

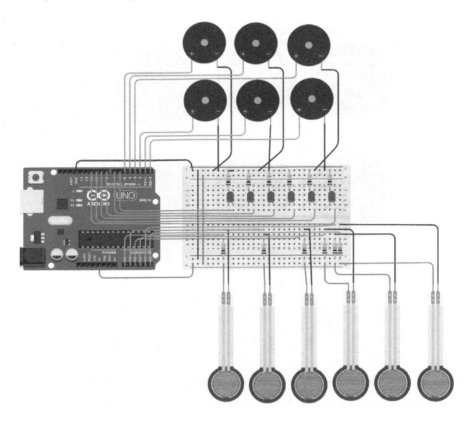

Great! Now we have successfully connected all components and can start programming our last project! Let's go!

8.3 Development of the program code

In this chapter we will again go step by step through the required programming.

You can try to create the complete programming of the project on your own. Use the same structure as for the previous projects. Also use the table with the frequencies and Tinkercad "tone" codes shown before. The solution can be found below.

Step 1:

In the first step we start - as usual - with the optional title block (to be found in the category "Notation") and the description: "mini piano". Since we don't need commands that are only executed on start, we can add an empty "on start" block. Of course, we could also simply omit this block.

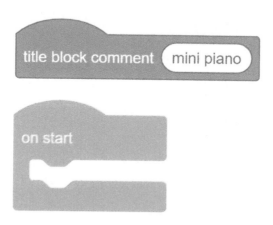

Step 2:

So in the second step we start here directly with the "forever" block, which executes our code in a loop. For the first tone, which should sound at piezo no. 1 (connection to pin 0 of the Arduino), we use an if-else condition, which says the following: If the read value of the force sensor (connection: pin A0) is greater than the threshold value 70, then on the one hand pin 6 should get the value "HIGH" (LED should light up) and on the other hand the piezo should play the tone C4 with the Tinkercad "tone" code 48 (frequency: 262 Hz). We start here, regarding the piano keys, on the left (key C4 on the piano) and then work our way step by step to the right to key A4 on the piano.

Sound	Frequency [Hz]	Tinkercad Code
C4	262	48

This then looks like this:

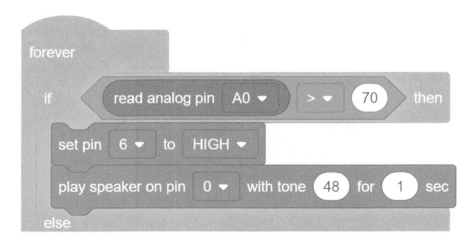

We now need the code for the case that the force sensor sends a measured value below the threshold value 70 to the Arduino (key is <u>not</u> pressed or released). We implement this code directly in the section "else":

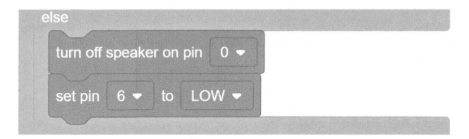

The speaker at pin 0 is switched off and the corresponding LED is also switched off.

Step 3:

Now we have to repeat step 2 for all force sensors or piezo buzzers. Here we basically only have to change the respective connections (force sensor, piezo, LED), as well as the Tinkercad "tone" code - depending on the tone. We add the code blocks directly under the previous ones. The structure remains identical. For the second tone D4, it would look like this:

Sound	Frequency [Hz]	Tinkercad Code
D4	294	50

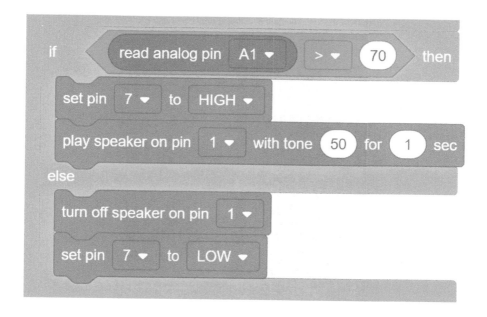

Step 4:

Now the remaining four keys with the following tones are missing:

Sound	Frequency [Hz]	Tinkercad Code
E4	330	52
F4	349	53
G4	392	55
A4	440	57

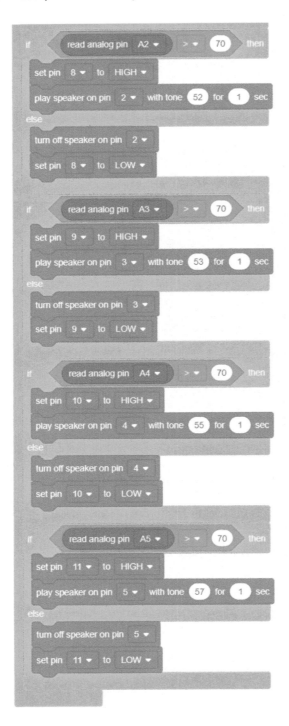

Complete program code:

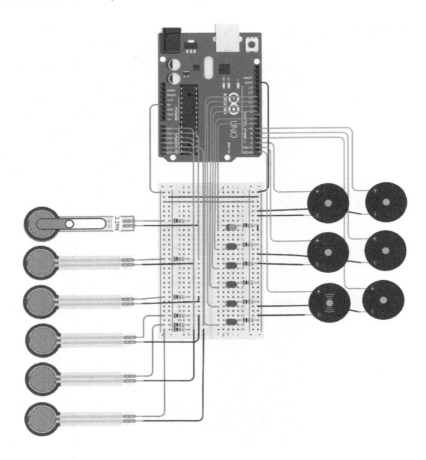

Perfect! Now we have also successfully completed this project. We can be proud of ourselves! Maybe you even managed it partially or completely on your own. Then you can be proud of yourself! Take a look at the next pages if you are not only interested in the Arduino, but also in other technical topics.

Closing words

Excellent!

You did it, you worked through the projects. That is a very good achievement!

In this book, I have tried to teach you how to create electronic schematics and program an Arduino using Tinkercad software through advanced and hands-on DIY projects. I hope I was able to reinforce your enthusiasm for electronics and programming. It should be a book that creates an understanding of the theoretical background knowledge and practical application.

Together we have accomplished quite a bit in this course! You can be justifiably proud of yourself if you've made it this far.

If you liked this book, I would be very happy if you leave me a rating and a short feedback as well as recommend the book to others! This will also help other people who are looking for a practical book like this.

Please also have a look at the following pages. Here you will find books on similar topics, the respective predecessor books to this book series, as well as a book on electrical engineering and Tinkercad in general. These books are ideal for an even more detailed introduction to the respective topics. Get your copies now!

Thank you very much!

Books on topics you might also like

All books are available online on the usual sales platforms. It's best to just search for the title, or feel free to visit my author page. Some of the books may not be published yet and will be released or found soon. Take a look at the books of your choice and your copy as e-book or paperback!

3D Printing:

CAD, FEM, CAM (3D Object Creation, Design, Simulation):

Electrical Engineering:

ELECTRICAL ENGINEERING Step by Step

Basics, Components & Circuits explained for Beginners

M.Eng. Johannes Wild

Photo voltaics 101

The hands-on beginner's guide for designing an on-grid or off-grid (stand-alone) PV system with battery storage for your home, RV, ...

M.Eng. Johannes Wild

ARDUINO STEP BY STEP

The Ultimate Beginner's Guide with Basics on Hardware, Software, Programming & DIY Projects

M.Eng. Johannes Wild

Arduino Projects with Tinkercad

Designing and programming Arduino-based electronics projects using Tinkercad

M.Eng. Johannes Wild

Arduino Projects with Tinkercad Part 2

Design & program advanced Arduino-based electronics projects with Tinkercad

M.Eng. Johannes Wild

Raspberry Pi | 101

The Ultimate Beginner's Guide with Basics on Hardware, Software, Programming & DIY Projects

M.Eng. Johannes Wild

Programming and other Software:

Excel 101

A Beginner's & Intermediate's Guide for Mastering the Quintessence of Microsoft Excel (2010-2019 & 365) in no time!

Johannes Wild

Tinkercad Step by Step

Learn how to easily create 3D objects (CAD), design electronic circuits and program with Tinkercad

M.Eng. Johannes Wild

CAD PROJECTS WITH TINKERCAD

3D-MODELS PART 1

Learn how to create advanced 3D objects with Tinkercad in an easy way

M.Eng. Johannes Wild

PYTHON Learn to Code Step-by-Step

The ultimate beginner's guide for an easy & instant start into programming with Python

M.Eng. Johannes Wild

There are also identical video courses for some of these books:

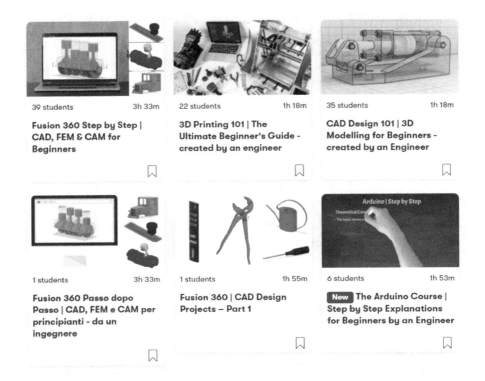

39 students   3h 33m

Fusion 360 Step by Step | CAD, FEM & CAM for Beginners

22 students   1h 18m

3D Printing 101 | The Ultimate Beginner's Guide - created by an engineer

35 students   1h 18m

CAD Design 101 | 3D Modelling for Beginners - created by an Engineer

1 students   3h 33m

Fusion 360 Passo dopo Passo | CAD, FEM e CAM per principianti - da un ingegnere

1 students   1h 55m

Fusion 360 | CAD Design Projects – Part 1

6 students   1h 53m

New The Arduino Course | Step by Step Explanations for Beginners by an Engineer

They are hosted on the learning website: skillshare.com

Be sure to use my following friends & family referral link to get a month of membership for free !

(I will get a little bonus if you choose to stay, so we will be both happy. Thanks in advance!)

https://www.skillshare.com/r/profile/Johannes-Wild/854541251

It is best to copy the link in your browser to access the free month !

Sign up today and deepen your knowledge!

Imprint of the author / publisher

© 2023

Johannes Wild
c/o RA Matutis
Berliner Straße 57
14467 Potsdam
Germany

Email: 3dtech@gmx.de

This work is protected by copyright

Thank you so much for choosing this book!

Made in the USA
Coppell, TX
03 September 2023

21136623R00069